LUAPULA
NORTHERN
Mokambo
Chitambo
Sakania
Ndola
Bwana Mkubwa
Fiwale Hall
Mission
Chondwe
Serenje
Kapiri Mposhi
R. Lukusashi
CENTRAL
Chibwe
R. Loangwa
Mkushi
Broken Hill
(Kabwe)
EASTERN
R. Lunsemfwa
Chisamba
MOZAM-
BIQUE

To Africa with Love

To Africa with Love

A Memoir of Arthur Cross of the United Missions in the Copperbelt of Zambia

by

Hugh G Cross

CROSS PATCH
EDITIONS

First published in 2001 by Cross Patch Editions
55 Slade Close, Ottery St Mary
Devon, EX11 1SX
United Kingdom

British Library Cataloguing in Publication Data
A catalogue record for this book is available from the British Library

ISBN 0-9539305-0-5

Typeset by Amolibros, Watchet, Somerset
This book production has been managed by Amolibros
Printed and bound by Professional Book Supplies, Oxford, England

Contents

Illustrations

Facing page 108

Foreword

by the Reverend Canon John C Houghton

Traditionally, as far back as the first century, the Christian church first established itself in the towns and cities, and then moved out to the "heath men", the heathen, in the rural areas.

The reverse happened in Northern Rhodesia for the simple reason that when Christianity was first preached in that country, there were no towns. The Church preceded the towns, as indeed it preceded government itself. But in due time, towns, mines and railways came, and then the first century pattern could be seen there too.

Starting in the late nineteenth century, a number of denominations began work in Northern Rhodesia. By 1920, the railway had reached Ndola and copper had begun to be mined at nearby Bwana Mkubwa. In February 1921, two young missionaries arrived at Ndola. They were Arthur Cross and Frieda Stern. They had volunteered for mission work in Lambaland at Kafulafuta, some forty miles from Ndola.

Thomas Hardy in his poem, "The Darkling Thrush", has a verse which, in part, says:

> "Or sign that they were bent
> By paths coincident
> Or being twin halves
> Of one august event".

The "paths coincident" which brought Arthur Cross and Frieda Stern to Lambaland in 1921 were that both of them were Baptists; both were Londoners; and both had responded to the call from the Reverend W A Phillips who had pioneered the work at Kafulafuta twenty years before. In other respects, however, their "paths coincident" had followed different routes.

Arthur Cross was born in Camberwell in 1898, the son of a Baptist Deacon and Sunday School Superintendent at Denmark Place Baptist Church. There Arthur was baptised in 1914 at the age of sixteen. Frieda, on the other hand, was the daughter of Julius Stern, a Jew from Leipzig who had emigrated to England. There, under the influence of Spurgeon, he became a Christian.

Julius married Louisa Annie Poole in 1899. She had formerly been a member of the C of E who had become a Baptist after being moved by the great evangelist, D L Moody.

These, then, were the parents of Frieda Stern. Julius took his family to South West Africa. There he engaged unsuccessfully in the diamond trade, and the family moved to Cape Town. By then, Frieda was aware of a call to missionary work. To prepare for it she went to America to train at Southern Baptist Seminary at Louisville, Kentucky.

The separate paths of Arthur and Frieda became rather more "coincident" in 1921 when it happened that Arthur arrived in Cape Town at the same time that Frieda returned from America. And both were in touch with the South Africa Baptist Missionary Society, ready to go to Northern Rhodesia to the Lambaland Mission at Kafulafuta. They were young and idealistic, but with much to learn in their new land.

Arthur Cross was not yet ordained. So in addition to learning the language and practising his vocation in a new environment, he had also to study theology and prepare for ordination. This he achieved successfully. By the end of his first six years at Kafulafuta, he was ordained on 27th February, 1927. That same year it was decided that Arthur and Frieda should move to Ndola.

By then the "paths coincident" had already made Arthur and Frieda "twin halves" of another "august event", for on

16th January 1923 Arthur and Frieda had married at Kafulafuta. The Baptist Missionary Society, chronically short of funds like all Missionary Societies, wrote to say: "Your combined stipends amount to £250. It is POSSIBLE that it may be increased to £275 IF NECESSARY"!

The year 1924 was climactic both for Northern Rhodesia as a territory and for Arthur Cross as a person. In 1924, the administration of Northern Rhodesia by the British South Africa Company ceased, and the country became a Protectorate under the British Crown with its own government – the Northern Rhodesian Government.

In 1924, too, Arthur was chosen to attend a meeting of the NR Missionary Conference at Kafue as a representative of the Baptist Church. He could not have realised how profound a difference that meeting would make to his own development, and to the crucial and pivotal role he would later play in inter-church relations, and in the wider field of Church-State affairs.

Arthur was deeply moved by the ecumenical nature of the gathering at Kafue of some thirty missionaries from some ten denominations. "Unity, not uniformity", he wrote, "was the keynote of the Conference, making for strength of character that worldly compromise can never engender." He was equally impressed by the fact that such a conference gave opportunity for Church and State to co-operate, for the great benefit of both.

Three years later, in 1927, at the next meeting of the General Missionary Conference Arthur Cross was made its secretary and he held that post until his untimely death in November 1945 at the early age of forty-seven.

Arthur's service as Secretary of the NR General Missionary Conference was invaluable because of the true spirit of ecumenism that he brought to it. Despite the wide range of denominational differences of the various churches, all could appreciate and respond to his sincerity. When he died memorial services were held for him in Lusaka, Mindolo, Ndola, Kafulafuta and at Mufulira. And the Mufulira Free

Church chose wisely when on the plaque erected there in Arthur's memory they inscribed those words from Chaucer:

> "He was a varray parfit gentil knight"

Understandably, the Roman Catholic Church was less able to participate as fully as other churches in following Arthur's lead, but it nevertheless recognised the invaluable and pivotal importance of his work. The Anglican Church in Northern Rhodesia had always valued its own catholic tradition, but it too valued all that Arthur was trying to do. In particular, as this memoir makes clear, the Anglican Bishop, Alston May, was always and consistently a staunch ally and supporter of Arthur Cross.

I first came to Northern Rhodesia as a mission priest early in 1942 and became aware at once of Arthur Cross and his invaluable role in the country's history. I attended the meeting of the NR General Missionary Conference at Chalimbana in 1944. That meeting was historic, not only as the last meeting of the old NR Missionary Conference, but also as the inaugural meeting of its replacement – the NR Christian Council. In one capacity or another, I was privileged to be a member of the executive of the Christian Council of Zambia (as it became) until I left the country in 1974.

Hugh Cross in this memoir to his father describes Arthur's journey back to England in 1945. It was the last such journey Arthur was to make. I can respond personally to the account Hugh gives us of that voyage, because as it happens I too was sailing from Cape Town to England in 1945, though not on the same ship. For me, it was my first leave from Africa.

The war in Europe was over, but not the war against Japan. So passages on ships were very hard to come by. So each of us, Arthur Cross and I, counting ourselves lucky to get a passage at all, sailed from Cape Town to England in 1945 – Arthur on the *Mauretania* and I on the *Durban Castle*, both of them peacetime liners which had become troop ships.

But I have left till last the true significance of Arthur Cross and the nature of his importance in Zambia's history. It explains why I am so glad this memoir has at last been written. We can regret that it was not written earlier and Hugh Cross explains how that came about. But at least, and at last, it is now written to take its place in the archives of Church and State in Zambia.

It all has to do with copper and the challenge with which the mining of copper confronted the churches. Ndola was just the "gateway to the Copperbelt" and fanning out from Ndola great copper mines and their attendant towns came into being. To them in their thousands, flocked Africans from every part of the country. And in also came many hundreds of white people, especially from South Africa.

From his earliest days at Kafulafuta, Arthur Cross recognised both the challenge and the opportunity that this great influx of people represented. In the space of a few years, an enormous industrial and sociological development was taking place. What should the churches do about it? It was an early part of Arthur Cross's realisation that it would make sense "not to do separately what we can do together". Could there not be a United Mission to the Copperbelt? So the letters UMCB became part of everyone's vocabulary. Of course, the individual churches and denominations would each do separately what they could. But could not their ministry be the more effective if they could join forces and share resources?

That was the kernel of Arthur Cross's vision. Gradually, and sometimes painfully, the idea took shape. Perhaps there might be a centrepiece for it all – a sort of UMCB Mission Station of a new kind, right in the heart of the Copperbelt? The name Mindolo began to be heard. The various churches were sounded out for their reactions and asked what they might be able to contribute in personnel and financial support.

Put like that, one might suppose that the idea would readily be accepted and implemented. But all this was happening in the middle of World War II. Mission Boards in Europe and South Africa needed to be consulted. Because of the war, recruitment was difficult – even impossible. Mission funds were even harder to come by, and arranging meetings in wartime meant that most of the work must be by correspondence. There was another dimension too – "unrest on the Copperbelt"...

Through it all, Arthur Cross clung to his vision. "Cometh the hour, cometh the man." Many rallied to his support, most notably Bishop Alston May of the Anglican Church and the Reverend J G Soulsby of the Methodist Church. In the end, these three – Cross, May and Soulsby, became the troika which drew the project forward to fruition.

In all this, Arthur Cross nursed no ambition to become himself the leader of the UMCB. But an increasing number of people thought that he was exactly the man for the job. Arthur Cross travelled to England in 1945 to attend meetings to review the work of the UMCB.

Alas, he fell ill and died in London before it could be done.

At the risk of extending this overly-long foreword there is one thing more to add. It is that Hugh, the son of Arthur Cross, has written this memoir of his father. And how apt that is, because it gives us a delightful example of how history can repeat itself, and an example too of the old saying – "Like father, like son".

I first knew Hugh Cross when he was a teenager in Lusaka. Our paths crossed many years later in Milton Keynes to which I had retired. To Milton Keynes came The Reverend Hugh Cross, Baptist Minister, to become the Ecumenical Moderator of the new "city" of Milton Keynes. Milton Keynes was created as a brand-new town in 1967. It was expected that by the end of the century its population would be 200,000 plus. What should the churches do in the face of this great challenge? Part of the answer was the creation of Christ the Cornerstone, to be not only a city-centre church but also a campus on which would be developed a whole range of projects and services.

And all this would be shared in by a fully ecumenical team of priests and ministers. And the Ecumenical Moderator would help to foster all this.

It is surely not irreverent to say that Arthur Cross must have rejoiced to see how his son had followed in his footsteps.

John Houghton

Preface

This book has been waiting to be written for over fifty years. When Arthur Cross died in November 1945, his widow, Frieda, felt strongly that a biography should be written because he had played a significant part in the life of the church and in the service of the nation, then Northern Rhodesia, now Zambia.

Frieda first asked a friend to do it and he agreed, although I suspect that he did so more out of friendship and love of Arthur and Frieda than out of a more considered belief that he would have the time to do it. Letters were sent out, and other means were adopted to seek the views and stories that would form the basis of the book. In addition, Frieda and the family passed over what letters they had, too. But the book did not materialise and the friend eventually admitted that, being a busy minister with many responsibilities, he had not the time to do the work.

At this point another friend volunteered to take on the task, and even began writing. A couple of draft chapters were completed before he, too, found the task beyond him.

Then the papers were bundled together into a parcel, and for many years lay untouched and unopened. Frieda grieved that the work had not been done, but no one she approached felt able to complete it.

My part in the project began when, in October 1998, at the end of a party celebrating the Golden Wedding Anniversary of my sister, Myra and her husband, the Reverend Dr Fergus Macpherson, Myra handed me the parcel (which had been given to her by our elder brother Howard) and told me I could do what I wished about it. When I opened the parcel at home and saw what it contained, I felt this was something I should attempt for the sake of both my parents.

The task has had its difficulties, not least of which has been the time lapse between my father's death and the start of the present project. Many of the people who would have been able to tell me stories or answer questions are now dead. No papers of my father's exist except such material as is in files in archives, which I have consulted. When my mother died in 1982 she left instructions that the letters my father had written to her should be destroyed unopened; a great loss to a biographer.

Yet there was material available to work on. I quote at length from two books that I have possessed for many years, *Christians of the Copperbelt* by Taylor and Lehmann[1], and *Towards Church Union in Zambia* by Peter Bolink[2]. It was at the point of opening the parcel that I suddenly realised that I had had in my possession for a number of years a file bearing the title in my father's handwriting, 'Copper Belt Proposals'. Its dating can be discerned by the fact that 'Copper Belt' was a form used until about 1936, and its contents at that point came alive for me. The file contained copies of correspondence between my father and the "London Committee", as well as some other letters. It is the one existing survivor of my father's papers, and I had never realised it before. It features greatly in the story that follows. During 1999, I was able to visit the library of the School of Oriental and African Studies in London and there delve into the archives of the International Missionary Council, which proved a mine of precious and interesting material.

---

1 Taylor, John V, and Lehmann, Dorothea (1961), *Christians of the Copperbelt*, London, SCM Press Ltd.

2 Bolink, Peter (1967), *Towards Church Union in Zambia*, Franeker, The Netherlands, T Wever

I asked my siblings for any material they might have, and each provided what they were able. Howard sent me the set of cased copies of *Lambaland* magazines, which my father had accumulated from his first going to Northern Rhodesia until his death. He also, along with Myra and Rosemary, wrote me a paper providing memories of my father. Each has been most helpful in filling in events and stories. I am especially grateful to Myra, whose encouragement has been unfailing, whose interest has been constant, and who typed and edited the raw manuscript and prepared it for publication. Representing the next generation in the family are my daughter, Kathleen, and son, Allan, to whom also I owe special thanks for reading the manuscript and making helpful suggestions which have improved the text considerably.

Naturally, in writing my father's biography I wished to include something about my mother and her family background, and if I lacked material about my father, there was even less about my mother. Then, two cousins in the United States, Dr Colin Sterne and the Rev Merold Stern, each the son of one of my mother's two brothers, were in touch with me and I took the opportunity to ask them for help. This they freely gave and I found it very helpful.

I am therefore indebted to many people, and I want to acknowledge that indebtedness, for without all these strands of information this would have been an impossible task. My thanks are due also to my wife, Doreen, for her active encouragement, for her tolerance and patience as I told her excitedly about the stories I was unfolding, and for her constant understanding and help when the going has been difficult – like losing some material from my word processor!

Finally, I wish to thank Jane Tatam of Amolibros who has helped me to publish the book.

To say this has been a labour of love is to understate the case. I have found in working on this book a growing closeness to my father that I was denied when he died in my sixteenth year. Not just, then, a labour of love, but one of immense joy and satisfaction. And pride, in being the son of such a man as my father.

Hugh Cross
Ottery-St-Mary, Spring 2000

CHAPTER ONE

Arrival in Northern Rhodesia

Five o'clock on a rainy morning in February 1921, the train from Cape Town steams into Ndola Station, near the border between Northern Rhodesia and the Belgian Congo. Eagerly peering out of the carriage window are two young people, Arthur Cross and Frieda Stern, for whom this is the first glimpse of the land where they are to work as missionaries.

Until a few weeks before they had never met, but both were new recruits to the Lambaland Mission of the South African Baptist Missionary Society. Travelling with them from the Cape was the Mission Superintendent, the Rev W A Phillips, a pioneering missionary who, with Mr Henry Masters, had begun the mission in that area twenty years previously.

In the early morning gloom, their eyes searched through the waiting crowd until they could dimly make out the features of a group of African men who had walked forty miles through the bush to meet them. This welcoming party would carry them and their luggage the forty miles back to the mission station at Kafulafuta, which was to be their new home. As soon as the new arrivals were spotted, there was a spontaneous rush forward to greet them and to carry their luggage to the place where camp had been made and where breakfast was soon prepared for them.

Ndola in 1921 was nothing like the bustling city it is today, with its university and its hospital and its busy trading centre. You could pitch tents there in those days. There was plenty of room, but already the town was beginning to grow. It stood beside a stream, and rose up a hill from the marshy ground near it. There were already houses of various kinds standing beside dusty red-earth roads. There were shops, too, where Frieda went to make some purchases before they set off into the bush. The town had even then become an important centre for provincial government, a trading post and the "rail head" for people living hundreds of miles out in the forests. Soon it would become the "Gateway to the Copperbelt", (*sic*, see Preface, pxiii) for copper was already being mined five miles south at Bwana Mkubwa, and other copper mines were then being prospected along the rich seam of copper-bearing rock that flowed across the border and joined the territories of Northern Rhodesia and the Katanga Province of the Belgian Congo (now the Democratic Republic of Congo). Arthur and Frieda would, in due course, become citizens of Ndola, and Arthur would eventually become a town councillor. But I am racing ahead of my story. We shall return to Ndola later, as they did.

Lambaland, as the rural area was called, was richly forested, and in those days was the home of a people called the Walamba; they called the country Ilamba. It covered an area of some 25,000 square miles. When our story begins, it was home not only to humans but also to a wide range of wildlife, including lions, leopards, elephants, and smaller animals like antelope and monkeys. Ndola had been a stopping place for the slave caravans, which had ceased to travel through the land only a few short years before. Still existing was the slave tree, a place where slaves were traded and from which they began their painful and sometimes fatal march towards the sea on the east coast of Africa two thousand miles away. Living in villages near Ndola were, even in the late 1920s, some of the old Swahili traders who had previously traded in slaves. The Walamba lived in small villages dotted throughout the forest. They had suffered terribly throughout the period when slavery was dominant, and still to some extent carried the memory of those times in their way of living and their responses to new people. It was to serve these people that the newcomers had arrived.

The lives of these two young missionaries were to be lived out in a beautiful land on the brink of huge changes that would bring rapid development of towns and modern industrial mining of copper, and an influx of thousands of workers, both black and white, from countries in Africa and beyond its bounds, to work in the mines. In consequence, others would follow to work in the ancillary commercial, industrial, agricultural and governmental infrastructure that was necessary to support life on the mines. The peaceful countryside of Lambaland would become a busy, populous area, where roads would be driven through the forests, new towns spring up and grow into cities, wildlife disappear, and a new style of urban living would replace the traditional, quiet, rural, agricultural landscape.

As Arthur and Frieda disembarked from the train that dark, rainy February morning in 1921, they could not begin to know what turbulent times lay ahead, or how their idealised dreams of missionary service in remote African bush were to be translated into the reality of being caught up in new ways of mission. The resources and training of their upbringing in Christian households in cities far from where they now found themselves would be taxed to the limit by the demands of the changes that were even then beginning to take place in this land to which they had committed their young lives in the service of Christ.

CHAPTER TWO

Beginnings

Arthur James Cross was born in Camberwell, south-east London, on 21st March 1898. His father, Thomas James, was a general builder. He was a Londoner. Arthur's mother, Eliza Annie Lathrop Snell, was of Devonshire extraction, in the south-west of England.

Arthur was one of five children born to Thomas and Eliza. Howard, the eldest, had died aged three years. Leonard was seventeen when he died in 1903. Winifred (Winnie) was born in 1892. Then came Arthur, and after him, the youngest, Kathleen (Kath), born in 1900. Family tradition has it that Eliza was heartbroken by Leonard's death, and became an invalid, dying nine years later, when the young Arthur was fourteen years old.

Childhood

Arthur was an adventurous young man, given to exploring. It is reported that, aged four, he was discovered in the signal box at the nearby railway station, claiming that he had merely gone to "have a look round". Two years later he was punished for climbing to the top of a telegraph pole. On another occasion, he went "scrumping" apples with a friend. Each tore his trousers, one in front and one behind, and since he dare not return home with torn trousers, he made a retreat to the friend's house to have them repaired. Some of his activity was mischievous, as for example putting forward the clock in church, which faced the preacher, so that he could be let out early. His hands were always busy making things, such as a "telephone" constructed from string and tin cans, and more adventurously, he and a friend made a boat, intending to sail it on a local lake, but before it was completed, his father had dissuaded him from sailing and gave him a fretwork set instead. These early adventures and demonstrations of practical ability with his hands were harbingers of Arthur's work as a missionary in making roads, directing the making of bricks and the building of houses, schools and churches, as well as supervising carpenters, builders, printers and other craftsmen.

Schooling

Arthur began school at the age of four, at Crawford Street London County Council School, where he remained until, at the age of eleven, he gained a scholarship which took him to St Olave's Grammar School, in the City of London. His time at St Olave's saw the beginning of friendships which stood firm over many years; one master in particular was still in touch with Arthur when he died in 1945.

His school reports from St Olave's ("STOGS" as he called it in his letters) reveal a dreamy boy, yet, in spite of that description, at the end of 1914 he gained first place in scripture, English literature and grammar. A study of his sermons reveals a sound basis in the classics, history, Greek and Latin. He was proud to have been a pupil at St Olave's, and in the four years he was there he was absent five times and late only twice. It was during his time at St Olave's that his mother died; is it fanciful to suggest that the apparent "dreaminess" and perhaps one of the absences were marks of the effect that occurrence had on him? His final report in 1914 speaks of his having "worked extremely hard", to which his headmaster added that "his career has been quite creditable", concluding with his best wishes.

Out to work, and war service

He left school to enter the realms of insurance at Lloyds in the City of London, where he had an unremarkable career before joining the Royal Navy in 1916 as a volunteer. After a short introductory course at Devonport, he was drafted as a signaller into the Dover Patrol with four others who had been with him at Devonport. He was assigned to HMS *Viking*, "one of our largest destroyers", and in a letter to his former schoolmaster he described an encounter with the enemy.

> "You can imagine what it is like tearing through the water as fast as your train in the morning, our eyes trying to pierce through the inky blackness of a moon-less night while the horizon ahead is fitfully lit up by the flashes of heavy firing. We hadn't the slightest idea what we had come out to meet, whether the High Seas Fleet or a few destroyers. The firing came from several different quarters and presently ceased so that it was nearly an hour before we met the enemy. The dark forms of ships were only just discernible when fire was first opened and they were uncomfortably close. The next few minutes were indescribable. A stay was shot away a few feet above our heads but otherwise we were not struck, although shells showered thickly around us. Soon their fire ceased and under cover of a smoke screen they made away."

A few days later Viking was hit by a heavy storm, and the whole bridge covering was washed away. Arthur, who was on the bridge at the time, was saved from being washed overboard by clinging to a wooden upright.

Christian influences

Thomas, Arthur's father, was a deacon and Sunday School superintendent at Denmark Place Baptist Church, nearby, and it was there that Arthur grew to faith, and where he was baptised on 26th July, 1914, and became a member of the church. The family home was one in which Christian values were practised, where family prayers were said, and where visitors were always welcomed. One such visitor had been the Rev W A Phillips, who had come to speak at the Denmark Place Church about his work in Lambaland. His accounts of his journeys and his work inspired the young Arthur, and sowed the seeds that later bore fruit in his offering to go to Africa to serve its people.

He owed much to the Sunday School teachers who taught him there, and one, Miss Margaret Lewis, recounted memories of him later on.

> "I remember that it was entirely due to Arthur that I began an extra class on Friday evenings – as well as the one on Sunday afternoons. He came to me once and said he and some of the others would like to study the Bible 'from the outside point of view'. So I had to turn to and read up a whole lot of stuff...I can remember prowling round the British Museum with him and seeking out Hittite inscriptions and many others – connected with our study. Arthur was a real friend to me – even in those far off days – and I can see in my mind's eye very clearly, the direct look from his grave young face as he would attempt, humbly almost hesitatingly but very directly to say exactly what he thought about some problem. And what a lovely humour he had. When Donald first came out one Sunday afternoon in long trousers – it was Arthur's voice I heard behind me saying to him, very quietly but positively: 'The Lord delighteth not in the legs of man' – and from one small boy to another that was rather delicious."

CHAPTER THREE

The Call to be a Missionary in Africa

The visits of the Rev W A Phillips to his home, and the accounts he gave of life in far away Lambaland stirred Arthur deeply, but it was not until he was in the navy during the First World War that he became aware of the call to missionary service. He prayed that if he survived the war he might find some avenue of service for Christ, and with thoughts perhaps of Lambaland, he wrote to his father on 6th June 1917, expressing his sense that he was being called to be ordained to the Christian ministry. There followed a fascinating correspondence between the young Arthur and his doting father.

It is a pity that we do not have the letters written by Arthur to his father, but some hints of their contents are revealed in those of Thomas to his son, "my only boy", as he lovingly calls him. On 9th June 1917 Thomas wrote to acknowledge a letter which "arrived this morning" but did not have time to reply fully to it, and wanted to think it through before making a more measured response. At that moment he wanted Arthur to "rest assured that I have neither word or thought of disapproval". He was absolutely clear that the call must come from God, and not either the desire of Arthur or his father. While the matter was under consideration, he wished Arthur to keep the matter between them, even though he gathered that Arthur had shared his feelings with at least one friend. Thomas wrote, "...but I am just praising God my Father that he has honoured me by putting such a thought into the heart of my only boy." The letter ends with the confidence that Arthur will "be worthy of your Darling Mother" and whether or not he should attain the end he had in view: "...may the desire to serve and follow Him Who loves us never grow fainter but rather increase." As we shall see, the desire did increase.

On 5th July, Thomas wrote a longer, more considered, letter to Arthur. He writes that he has not had the opportunity previously to give long consideration to the question of Arthur's sense of call, but significantly uses the phrase "...provided that it is as you say a distinct call of God why then of course there can be no refusal... ." The words "as you say" give a clue to what Arthur had written. He cautions the young man, "...there is no need to be hasty..." and reminds him that he has a task in hand which must be completed, namely, his service in the Royal Navy. The older man is aware of the dangers Arthur must encounter, and in a moving passage describes his feelings.

"When you left home and especially after you joined your ship I just gave you over into the hands of a loving God and Father, if it was His will to spare you to return to me and those who love you, well! but if not – I had just resigned you to His will and still all would be well." He then talks about his own suffering and the losses he has already sustained, the greatest of which was that of his wife, Arthur's mother, adding, "...and should you be taken from me it would be one more added sorrow and grief – but – I have been learning and am still learning that it is good to be called to pass through suffering and sorrow if it be to glorify the God who has called me to serve him and serve him by these."

I have quoted him fully in order to show the kind of man he was, and how the strength of his own faith must have gone largely towards developing Arthur's own sense of calling.

Another passage in the letter gives another hint of what Arthur had written, and in response Thomas pours out his own soul to his son:

> "You have touched a deeper chord than you think when you refer to yourself as my youngest boy – years have passed away since your dear brothers were taken from your Mother and me but time cannot efface their memory and they are more dear to me than I can tell… . But meantime you are spared to me and I pray you may be still. What greater joy can I have than to know my dear son is giving his best for Him Who has given us all?"

He then turns to "practical" matters, advising Arthur that he was released by his employers to enter the navy, and that when "the end of this terrible strife" comes he would be returning to their employ. At that point it would be necessary to see "how things shape themselves", but for the present no good could come by opening up the issue of Arthur's call.

One further letter exists in this correspondence, but it is more difficult to interpret. Written on 24th May 1918 in response to one from Arthur, it tells how Thomas has been extremely busy and often physically tired, but is in good health. It goes on to record his own prayers for his son, as well as the prayers of Arthur's mother during her long illness before she died. Turning to the "more immediate practical part of your letter", he writes, "My dear boy I am most grateful for your thoughtfulness and may that be a quality that will remain with you all the way through… ." The puzzle is to know what the "thoughtfulness" refers to, though the context suggests that perhaps Arthur was concerned that, his father growing older and he being the only son, taking up the call to missionary service would deprive the old man of someone who might be able to help provide for him in his old age, or be able to take on the home, while Winnie went out to work.

Whatever it was, eventually Arthur returned to Lloyds after the war, and then later on followed his calling to Africa, with the blessing of his father.

CHAPTER FOUR

Frieda

Frieda Stern's father, Julius, was a Jew from Leipzig, who emigrated from there to England as a young man. He became a Christian under the influence of the great nineteenth-century Baptist preacher, Charles Haddon Spurgeon, who then drew large crowds to the Metropolitan Tabernacle at the Elephant and Castle in south London. As a consequence of this change of faith, his parents disinherited him and, in orthodox fashion, held a funeral service for him, making the break formal. There appears to have been a later reconciliation, but little is known about it except that it happened.

Julius was an active worker with the London City Mission, and earned his living for a time as head of the tourist bureau of the Great Eastern Railway at Liverpool Street Station. Part of his work was to conduct parties of tourists to mainland Europe, where his knowledge of French, German, Italian and some Spanish was useful. A kind and affectionate man, he once asked a Salvation Army girl to kiss him, which she agreed to do on condition he gave up consuming alcohol. He promised, was kissed, and kept his promise for thirty years, when he went back on his word for a time. Julius fell in with some business partners who practised some shady dealings, which resulted in his imprisonment for six months, while strongly protesting his innocence.

He married Louise Annie Poole, a convert of the great evangelist, D L Moody. Previously a member of the Church of England, Louise became a Baptist after her conversion. Her father was a gardener, and her elder brother, Henry T Poole, was a builder in Woodford, Essex, where Louise and Julius lived and where their three children, Frederick (Fred), born 1892, Julius (Jack), born 1895, and Frieda Annie, born 1899, first saw the light of day. Following the prison sentence the family moved to South West Africa in 1902, where Julius speculated in the diamond trade with little success. They then moved to the Cape, and made their home in Claremont, where Frieda grew up.

Becoming aware of a call to missionary service, Frieda went to the United States of America to train at the Southern Baptist Seminary at Louisville, Kentucky, and arrived back in Cape Town about the same time that Arthur arrived with Mr Phillips from England. Frieda was a woman of ability and determination. She worked hard among the women and girls at Kafulafuta, and took her part in going out "on trek" into the surrounding villages. Her health suffered and she had frequent bouts of malaria to contend with in the early days at the mission station. The move later to Ndola did not entirely eradicate Frieda's weakness.

The Wedding

While they were in Cape Town, Frieda and Arthur were mercilessly teased about going up to Lambaland together, and it was confidently said that they would marry, but each emphatically denied any romantic interest in the other, let alone marriage. Eighteen months later, the Secretary of the South African Baptist Missionary Society (SABMS) wrote to Arthur "to convey to you and Miss Stern the very hearty consent and congratulations of the Committee on your engagement". Later in the letter he continued, "You will of course be continuing your studies under the (Ministerial) Education Committee, while we leave it to Miss Stern to do as she pleases." Their courtship was conducted on a mission station where they were two of the four single missionaries in residence, and when taking a walk together they were always chaperoned for the sake of propriety!

Propriety seems to have been a major deciding factor when deciding on a date for the marriage. Arthur wrote to the Missionary Society in November 1922 making a strong case for the mission superintendent, the Rev W A Phillips "...having at the earliest possible date a period of real rest..." adding, "I can personally bear witness to the fact that Mr Phillips's last furlough contained no rest for him at all, rather it was a time of strenuous activity." The reply from the SABMS was to approve Mr Phillips's holiday, but this created a problem. Arthur and Frieda would be left on their own at Kafulafuta. The committee, very sympathetic to the "...desire of Miss Stern and yourself to be married, and while heartily approving of it..." was of the opinion that it would be wise "...for your own sakes if this took place before Mr Phillips leaves on holiday. The Committee," the letter went on, "gives this advice solely for your own sakes and for the sake of the work in the eyes of the natives: we fully realise that your position on the station would be difficult otherwise."

The wedding took place in the Kafulafuta Church at twelve-thirty p.m. on Tuesday, 16th January 1923, described by Miss Olive Doke as "the first of its kind ever held in the building". Two or three times the arrangements had had to be altered because of difficulties in procuring the necessary legal documents from Livingstone (then the capital of Northern Rhodesia), but eventually the papers and the ring arrived and the wedding went ahead. Mr Phillips conducted the ceremony, Miss Doke was bridesmaid, a "Mr A K Young of Ndola" was best man, and the ring-bearer was six-year-old Fanny, daughter of one of the senior African workers. Music was provided by a gramophone, since the only organist was also bridesmaid! The service, conducted both in Lamba and English, began with the hymn "Let us with a gladsome mind" sung in Lamba, and ended with "Come Thou fount of every blessing". The wedding breakfast was held in Mr Phillips's home, while "a good feed" was provided for the seventy or so people from the villages and the mission who had attended the ceremony. Afterwards Arthur and Frieda spent a brief honeymoon at Chondwe Farm, some miles south of Ndola, at the invitation of its owner, Mr Morris.

Prior to their marriage, the combined stipends of the happy couple amounted to the princely sum of £250 per annum, which the missionary society proposed raising to £275 from the date of the wedding.

CHAPTER FIVE

Lambaland, 1921–1927

The journey from Ndola to the mission station at Kafulafuta, a distance of some forty or so miles, took two days. The missionaries were carried for part of the way in *machilas,* hammocks slung on poles carried by two bearers.

Arthur described the arrival there in this way,

> "It was between 3 and 4 p.m. when we reached Katanga's village, which lies only two miles from the Mission Station. As we get near to the Station we can hear the shouts of schoolboys, until round a bend in the path appear Mr and Miss Doke, followed by a crowd of boys who have come out to greet us. With great excitement and glee, we are escorted to the Mission Station fifteen to twenty acres of sloping ground, well laid out with avenues of tall aloe trees, and the red houses with their thatched roofs, all symmetrically arranged, and the red brick Church school in the centre of things, all forming a very pleasing sight. Added to this is the surrounding country of charming character – but words of mine can give you little idea of the physical beauty of the place. Really, 'every prospect pleases.' "

Within those "fifteen to twenty acres" of land that comprised the mission station at Kafulafuta, there was an orchard growing citrus fruit, fields where maize and millet were grown for use on the station, a dispensary at various times the responsibility of a qualified nursing sister, a printing press where school books and other materials for use in church were printed, brick kilns and a saw pit to provide building materials, as well as the houses and offices used by the missionaries and the African staff, the girls' and boys' boarding schools, and the church/school, already mentioned, at the centre. At first the only approach was along narrow paths from the rail head at Ndola, but later a main road was built by the government from Ndola to Luanshya Mine, and Arthur was responsible for driving a road through the eleven miles or so of bush that separated Luanshya from the mission.

Life for the missionary in those days involved periods of touring on bicycle or foot through the forests to the villages in the surrounding area. Many of the villages had schools, but some lacked this facility either because there was no teacher available or because the headman or the people were unwilling to establish one. Sometimes there would be a failure of the harvest, and this would mean that the missionary would defer a tour until the people had food for themselves and could offer it to the carriers and the missionary. Arthur recounted at one time a tour he made when only sweet potatoes were available, and it explained why ever afterwards he had an aversion to the vegetable, having had to eat it for every meal for ten days.

It was part of the missionary's work to make provision for food for the carriers who would accompany her or him on tour. Arthur, although he had served in the Royal Navy, had never been trained to use a rifle or shotgun, nor the skills required of the hunter, and Olive Doke recorded the fact that she taught him to hunt to obtain meat for the carriers. She recalled how she set off with Arthur early one morning, having decided not to try to shoot antelope, of which several would be needed to feed the carriers, but rather to shoot a hippopotamus. They walked through the bush to the confluence of the rivers Kafulafuta and Kafuwu, which was not too far from the mission. Creeping quietly across the open ground near the rivers they saw two hippos, one fully submerged in the water and the other lumbering out onto the river bank. Waiting until the beast turned its head in their direction, Olive squeezed the trigger on her rifle and shot it through its left eye, explaining afterwards to Arthur that one had to aim for the eye since the skin was too thick for a bullet to penetrate successfully. The animal dropped to the ground, but the hunters, instead of going immediately to inspect their kill, lest the other animal should attack them, returned to the mission and called out the carriers to come and butcher the beast, which they did by climbing inside when they had cut a large enough hole in its side and had removed all the meat on the carcass. There is no record of Arthur killing in this way, but no doubt he had to shoot buck when on tour to feed his porters.

Disease and sickness were frequently encountered. Kafulafuta Mission itself was situated on an unhealthy site near the confluence of the rivers Kafulafuta and Kafuwu, with the resultant endemic malaria from the mosquitoes which bred there. Leprosy was met often, and in the records are stories of people like Paul, who, in spite of the disabilities he suffered from the ravages of the disease, effected a significant ministry as an evangelist, and who managed the mission station on a number of occasions when the missionaries were away.

Heartbreaking stories occur throughout the literature of those early missionary years as Arthur, Frieda and the others encountered sad cases of sickness and disease which they were unable to do anything about. On his first trip solo round the villages, Arthur recounts how a woman brought to him a baby.

> "We were about to leave the village when I was apprised of the presence of a woman who wished me to see her baby who was ill. The mother came

forward bearing in her arms a tiny mite wasted and thin, with a look of pain on its face that I shall not easily forget. It was as if the few weeks of its acquaintance with the world had been weeks of agony…as I looked at this rough woman tenderly holding her baby and trying to soothe its peevish moans, I thought how, if the Saviour were here, it would be said, 'He had compassion upon her', and with one touch He had restored the little sufferer; and I longed to be able to do the same. Was it merely, as some say, the lack of faith on my part that precluded this ability? Or is it a matter of God's inscrutable purposes in this age that the healing touch should not be amongst the credentials of His messengers? We had prayer and I commended the mother and child to Him Who once was a 'Man of sorrows and acquainted with grief;' and may I confess that that prayer was a trial of faith to me, and I went away sad. This instance stands out most vividly, for it occurred when I was visiting the villages alone for the first time, but it may be multiplied by as many times as there are villages within our reach, for even the smallest villages have sick and afflicted. Not that the proportion is any greater here than at home, but here, where there is no privacy, and seclusion is impossible, one sees much that at home would be hidden from public sight behind the walls of a benevolent institution or in the castle of the Englishman's home."

Annually, in September or October, a conference was held at Kafulafuta, lasting two or three days, to provide spiritual nourishment to people from the villages round about. Some of those who attended walked for several days to be there. Participants slept in the school dormitories, and food was provided communally. Addresses were given by the missionaries and some African evangelists, and a service of baptism was usually held towards the end. A closing Communion service was the occasion for welcoming into church membership those who had been baptised, before they began the long journey home to their villages. Even after Arthur had moved on to serve at Ndola, and later when he moved to Mindolo, he would still return to these annual events to share in the preaching and teaching. Evidently he regarded them as important occasions, to be enjoyed, and to provide an opportunity to meet with people whom he loved and for whom he was a beloved pastor.

Kafulafuta was to be the home of Arthur and Frieda for the next six years, and in a letter to the South African Baptist Missionary Society, dated the 24th May 1923, Arthur wrote, "Our hearts and lives are wrapped up in our work here, and here is where we want to remain and to be used in God's service." This was repeated in August that year. They were in South Africa with Frieda's parents, when he wrote, "our own earnest desire is to return thither (to Kafulafuta) in January...we are extremely hopeful that God willing, we may return to the place which we regard as our home... ."

Home it certainly was for those few years. Immediately they arrived, they became immersed in the life of the mission station and of the people for whom it existed, taking their share of work on the station and of touring the district. Each contributed articles to *Lambaland*, the missionary magazine published in England for supporters of the mission. Those articles reveal something of the enthusiasm and joy that inspired their efforts, and in the earlier editions, one reads again and again of new experiences and, in Arthur's case, vivid descriptions of the country and its people.

It was at Kafulafuta where they married, and to Kafulafuta that they brought their first infant, Arthur Howard, who spent the first four years of his life there. That it was the place of hard labour and frustration is also part of the story of their sojourn at Kafulafuta.

The missionary and the missionary society

How the Lambaland Mission came under the auspices of the South African Baptist Missionary Society is a story of courage and faith and is well worth telling for its own sake – but not here. The mission was ceded to the SABMS in May 1914, by the Nyasa Industrial Mission, which up till then had employed the two pioneers, the Rev W A Phillips and Mr Henry Masters. The inspiration for the acquisition of the mission came about through the death, on his journey back from viewing the situation, of the Rev J J Doke, whose son, Clement, and daughter, Olive, soon joined the mission staff.

At the point when Arthur Cross and Frieda Stern arrived at Kafulafuta, Clement Doke was about to leave because his health was not up to staying at Kafulafuta. His wife's health had suffered badly and she had already returned to South Africa. Clearly, although the society employed these and other missionaries, it had no clear policy worked out regarding the terms of their employment. Correspondence shows that decisions about intervals between furloughs had not been formally taken, but were made "on the hoof". Similarly, it appears that what salaries should be paid, were decided on the basis of what funds were available, rather than on regular payment at fixed levels. Because Arthur raised these issues in correspondence the committee was obliged to regularise its employment policy.

Arthur wrote to the General Secretary, the Rev J Edgar Ennals, on 28th February 1921, acknowledging his appointment as "a Missionary on Probation" together with the receipt of "a copy of the Bye Laws of the Committee, also copy of the Constitution of Native Churches". His letter of appointment clearly spoke of his salary being £160 per annum, and Arthur's letter refers to "terms and conditions". Yet in a very brief space of time there was a series of letters relating to furloughs of staff, and the admission of the general secretary in a letter of 4th April 1923 that "we have gone on hitherto with arrangements for furlough in a somewhat hand to mouth manner", and the need to "get into a regular order so that our missionaries can reckon on their holidays and the society can estimate its probable expense and also arrange its staffing".

In November 1922, twenty-one months after Arthur arrived at Kafulafuta we find him, as we have already seen, writing to the SABMS General Secretary, "...speaking for the two lady missionaries as also for myself...on Mr Phillips's behalf upon the subject of his much needed change and rest". The reply from Dr Clem Doke, on behalf of the committee, was to sanction Mr Phillips taking his leave.

The letter from Dr Doke gives a hint that Arthur was even then well versed in the Lamba language, for Doke writes thanking him, "in my private capacity" for a letter he had sent in mid-November on the question of phonology (the study of the system of sounds) in Lamba. Doke admits a weakness in the phonology chapter in his Lamba *Grammar*, and says that he needs to have "a few weeks up in Lambaland again to study the phonetics". Doke was by now Professor of Bantu Languages at Witwatersrand University and had acquired a doctorate since leaving the mission.

Just before Frieda and Arthur's wedding took place a further letter arrived from South Africa, conveying the good wishes of the "Northern Committee" as it was called, and asking for a date for the event. It went on, "As to stipend you must leave that to our next full Committee to deal with... . Your combined stipends amount to £250. It is possible that it may be increased to £275 if necessary. What do you think? We want to do the best for you and for the Society in its need." So Frieda's stipend before they were married was £90 per annum.

But the question of furloughs loomed large. Phillips duly went on leave, having discussed furloughs with the others. It had been agreed that he would speak to the Northern Committee when he was in South Africa. The people in the field had agreed that the Crosses would take leave at the same time as Miss Doke, in mid-1923. Phillips had recognised that this arrangement would leave him alone at Kafulafuta while the others took leave, but he "himself was anxious that his being here without help and companionship for nine months should not stand in the way of arrangements for furlough". The alternative was to appoint "another white worker which under present financial conditions seemed a possibility too remote to be considered".

On 15th March, Arthur wrote to Mr Ennals, at SABMS headquarters, of their dismay at receiving a letter from Mr Phillips, while on leave in South Africa, "giving us to understand that, subject to the General Committee's approval we were not to be granted furlough until June 1924". The next mail brought no official confirmation of the committee's decision, and, "after much thought and much prayer in which we have both committed our future to God earnestly desiring to do His will alone", they had decided to make an approach to Ennals, asking him to intercede on their behalf with the General Committee for the furlough arrangements to stand. The urgency was that, fully expecting to be on furlough late in the year, Frieda was then in the early stages of pregnancy, the baby being expected in early November. "Don't you see the difficulty," Arthur wrote, "...under present circumstances it is imperative that at least the first little one should come during a furlough—not too early, and not too late. We had prayerfully to plan ahead and we did."

The committee had wanted to fix the furlough intervals at about three and a half years, and the missionaries agreed that that would be a good plan, but in the present instance it was not a good idea. The Crosses were mindful of the fact that two years and four months was rather a short first term, but "fever has not left her (Frieda) alone altogether and the past two years have been trying to her in many ways". Furthermore, he wrote, "...if furlough is for the preservation of the missionaries' health rather than for the mending thereof, it is not too short." They wished to be reasonable, and, if the committee so decided, they were prepared to stay on, "adequate provision being made for the safe arrival of the little one". Such a proposition would be a difficult one, however, because not only health considerations, but also expense had to be taken into account. If the committee decided that they should be separated at this crucial time, the complication arose that neither of them had a home to go to in South Africa. Ennals responded by undertaking to lay Arthur's letters before the committee, and remarking how much he appreciated the tone of the letters.

The next letter from Ennals was not appreciated. He reported, on 15th May, that the Northern Committee had decided to refer the matter to the General Committee on 21st June. That meant a further delay in decision, which was bearable, but his next sentence received a very dusty reply. He said, "I am to get medical opinion in the meantime as to the effects of quinine under the circumstances [of pregnancy]." He did, however, authorise Frieda being sent south in the meantime if that seemed necessary. Frieda's health clearly had been a cause for concern for some time, and Arthur wrote on 24th May that he was taking her to Ndola to catch the next train going south.

His letter continued, "It is no use disguising the fact that my wife has had a tremendous lot of low fever since coming up here – she has scarcely ever been free from it. Last Nov. she had dysentery and influenza which necessitated her keeping her bed for over eight weeks. And now for the last nine weeks fever and sickness have forced her to spend most of the time in bed with an occasional respite." They were not wanting to convey the impression of panic. It was simply that Frieda's physical well-being called loudly for furlough, and "by getting away from malaria now (as we expected she would get away) she will recruit health and be none the worse." He reiterated the fact that they both were committed to the work in Lambaland.

Then comes the response to Mr Ennals' report that he was to consult a doctor about quinine's effects on a pregnant mother-to-be. "May I," Arthur wrote, "just refer to one point in your letter which amazes me. I cannot understand the Committee commissioning you to consult a Dr. about quinine. How can any doctor who has never seen and knows nothing about Mrs Cross know how quinine affects her! Also it hardly reflects confidence in us or in the medical advice we have sought." Arsenic had apparently been recommended as an alternative to quinine, but had not been available. He continued that his application to accompany Frieda south still stood, and evidently he received permission to go. Arrived in South Africa, Frieda's health began to improve, though not before she had been examined by a doctor who reported to the committee as a result, but in whom Arthur and Frieda had "very good reason to be dissatisfied". Under a new doctor at the sanatorium where Frieda's confinement was to take place, better results were achieved. In due course, not in early November but on 2nd December 1923, Arthur Howard was born without complications. He has always been known as Howard because, in the excitement of registering his birth, Arthur put the names in the wrong order!

Staying in Cape Town was an expensive business, and there are indications that finances were precarious to say the least. In sending his congratulations on Howard's birth, Mr Ennals mentioned this and suggested that the sooner they could go north again, allowing for Frieda's health, "the better for finance as well as the work". But when it came to them going north, a new set of complications were triggered. An application in early January, 1924 for £25 for their rail fare to Ndola, met with a refusal from the Treasurer of the SABMS. He could not issue a cheque without the authority of the committee, he said, and furthermore he considered it "injudicious" for Frieda to travel to Kafulafuta during the rainy season "and in the absence of any other European woman on the Station". Because of the society's finances being in "such a state" he was unhappy paying out £25 if in the next few months he would have to pay out the same amount to bring her back south. He covered himself by saying that, of course he had no inside knowledge of things at Kafulafuta or in the family, or, indeed, "of the opinion of the Committee, but merely as the Treasurer". Letters and telegrams went back and forth for several days until Arthur wired the general secretary requesting him to authorise the treasurer to pay out the money, and saying that he had borrowed the fare and bought the tickets for their return on 23rd January. The reply came back, "Northern Committee reluctantly acquiesces."

That it was difficult to make ends meet financially is clear. There is a letter from the accountant, Mr P Maschke, written in November 1924, which takes this up very delicately. He had apparently written earlier and Arthur had replied, apologising for brevity. Maschke had simply wanted to know "how you are keeping and getting on". He continues, "Now in regard to your own material sustenance, be not offended, dear Mr and Mrs Cross, if I speak very plainly. Your first duty, as I see it, would be to earnestly endeavour to make ends meet with your present salaries. This, no doubt, you have honestly sought to do. Having failed, your second duty – not only to yourself but also to the Committee – would be to place your circumstances frankly before the Committee. I know funds are low, but I am convinced that the Committee does not want any of our missionaries to be in 'real distress'. You cannot get away from this, and there is nothing humiliating about the matter. You would not be asking for luxuries nor for charity. It would be humiliating to the Committee and also to the Society, which they represent, to find one of their Missionaries in real want. Do not let the matter go on any longer, but lose no time in taking the necessary steps to make them aware of your need." Which they did in January the following year, asking simply that their stipends should "revert to the figures obtaining before the reduction in 1921 of thirty shillings [£1.50] and twenty shillings [£1.00] respectively".

In due course, they received cheques of £12.6.8 (£12.34) and £8.10.0 (£8.50), presumably "back-pay". In May, their joint stipends were raised to £180 per annum, although the society had a heavy overdraft, and was asking the supporters in England to help raise the extra amount.

This matter of poor finances hung over the missionaries and their work, and is referred to time and again in letters and publications. Many times, Arthur or Frieda or one of the others, writing in *Lambaland* magazine expressed the frustration of the shortage of missionary staff, and remarked on how much more could be done with more hands to do it. It was not the case that they ignored their African colleagues, for there was a programme of training and bringing on their African co-workers throughout the period. But, while these were being encouraged and brought on, there was still more work than enough to keep them all occupied.

After Phillips retired there was an incident in 1926 when a couple of missionaries were promised, who had had considerable experience elsewhere in missionary service. They were expected with great enthusiasm, but at the last minute the arrangement fell through. Judging by a letter from the general secretary to him in June 1927, Arthur had apparently fired off a broadside (as Arthur might have described it, having served in the navy) at the committee's failure to find someone. Mr Ennals wrote that the committee had sent letters off to Baptist Colleges and the Baptist Missionary Society in England seeking candidates for Lambaland. He went on, "May I point out however that your castigation of the committee for inaction in the matter, was wholly unmerited. We did not know till after the Executive that the Joneses were not coming, and they had actually been appointed." Arthur was duly penitent, though he replied, "Your rebuke for what you call my castigation of the Committee is gentler than I deserve, but I can't say 'sorry' honestly if it has had anything to do with the letters to England! Your letter has put a new spring in our step."

But the letters to England seemed to have no effect. Instead, a young man from one of the churches at the Cape, then an employee of South African Railways, took leave and journeyed up to Lambaland to have a look at it, deciding as a result to offer himself for missionary service there. The missionaries on the spot must have indicated to the society that they would not be happy if he were to be appointed. No letters exist, but there are references to them. On the train on his way home from the Baptist Union Assembly in Cape Town in September 1927, Mr Ennals wrote to Arthur, "We interviewed Mr Skinner as an Executive and were much impressed by him in a very difficult situation. The result is the rather surprising one perhaps that the Committee quite unanimously decided to accept him as a missionary for Lambaland." He continued, "Now I need hardly plead that though this is not in accord with the expressed wish of you all in Lambaland that you will accept the situation frankly and keep Mr Skinner from feeling there is any latent opposition to him in the work. I think you must take his appointment as an answer to your prayers though not in the way expected. It may need grace for him as well and perhaps more than for you, but I feel sure that you will be given grace sufficient if you see fit. I have advised him not to try to find out the source of the disapproval and to act as if there were none and it will be necessary for you all to treat him in the same way." One wonders what happened to the "spring in the step" referred to above in view of this new development.

For the record, it appears that Skinner arrived in January 1928. In April 1929, he married Miss Barbara Beyers, and they "proceeded almost immediately" to Kafulafuta. Mrs Skinner was a trained nurse, and made a welcome addition to the staff in being able to provide medical services through the dispensary. However, the relief was short-lived, and the Skinners returned to South Africa in September or October 1930. The cause of their leaving the field appears to be Mrs Skinner's nervous breakdown, and the committee decided that they should be withdrawn, hoping that the "door of opportunity will open for them in some other sphere". Once more, Arthur, Frieda and Olive Doke were left to carry on the work.

Ordination

While carrying out the strenuous work of a missionary, Arthur was obliged also to study for his ordination examinations. Reference has already been made to the seriousness with which these studies were regarded by the missionary society. That he was a keen student, eager to learn, can be judged by the fact that, during the voyage out from England, Arthur had begun a course in UwuLamba under the tutorship of Mr Phillips. He studied hard and learned well, remarking later that he was pleased to be able to understand some of the conversations Phillips had with African people on the journey up from the Cape.

His ordination studies were as full as if he had attended a theological college. The course included introductions to the Old and New Testaments and detailed studies of particular books in each, church history, doctrine, Baptist principles, comparative religion and experimental religion, systematic theology, philosophy, apologetics, ethics, Greek, homiletics and the production of two sermons under examination conditions. Throughout his studies he achieved never less than eighty per cent and in two cases ninety-five per cent for his examinations, so qualifying with honours. It was reported that in the case of one set sermon he had been given the wrong text for the topic set! The examiner wrote, "In the sermon he was at a great disadvantage. The question as written was: 'Aim, through John 5:18 to lead souls into light and life.' I meant John 5:24. How the mistake occurred I do not know. But difficult as the process was Mr Cross got there. I award him 80/100."

Awarding Arthur ninety-five per cent for a paper on Isaiah, the examiner remarked, "There is nothing slipshod in Mr

Cross's work." Nothing slipshod underscores the attention to study that Arthur applied. He wrote in September 1925, "I now regret that I cannot hope to have more than the first three subjects ready for examination in November. This is due almost wholly to the pressure and distracting nature of the work during the past months. These studies are a real joy to me and my regrets in having to write thus are deep and real. I am sure you believe in me enough not to wish me to enter into details in substantiating the above reason, but should you for official purposes require something fuller I will write again, or better, Mr Phillips." In 1926, Arthur was appointed superintendent of the mission in succession to W A Phillips, who retired on health grounds, and it is clear that even before this Arthur must have been carrying some of Phillips's load.

Arthur was ordained to the Baptist ministry in the King William's Town "Native" Baptist Church on the afternoon of Sunday, 27th February 1927.

The year 1927 was also significant because of two other major events in the life of Arthur and Frieda Cross. The first was that they moved from Kafulafuta to Ndola for reasons we shall explore later on, and lived at first in a small house in the "Native Location". The second significant event was the birth in that tiny house of Myra Anne, a sister for Howard, on 30th May.

CHAPTER SIX

A Significant Moment

An event occurred in 1924 that was to shape the future of Arthur's ministry. He was chosen to attend the meeting of the Northern Rhodesia General Missionary Conference representing the South African Baptist Missionary Society missionaries.

On 1st April 1924, the territory of Northern Rhodesia ceased to be administered by the British South Africa Company (the "Chartered Company" of Cecil Rhodes's founding) and became a Protectorate under the British Crown. The event ushered in a new relationship between missions and colonial government in the territory, and the meeting of the General Missionary Conference had been brought forward a year earlier than usual to take account of this new start. Government was represented at the conference by some high officials, and greetings were received from the governor and other senior members of the administration. The meeting was held at Kafue in the centre of the territory.

Arthur's account of the Conference, written for *Lambaland* of October that year, clearly shows several important factors in his own personal development.

He was clearly affected by the ecumenical nature of the gathering, and the international aspect of the participants – "...the Missionaries themselves," he wrote, "British, American, French, Dutch, Swiss, Polish – all one in Christ Jesus, and for the highest interest of the native. Ten denominations were represented... . Unity, not uniformity, was the keynote of the Conference, making for strength of character that worldly compromise can never engender."

Second, he was impressed by the collaboration of government and missions, writing, "...The hearts of all the missionaries were gladdened when they saw that the first Order in Council instructed the new Governor to promote to the utmost of his power religion and education among the natives."

A large part of his report is devoted to an address given by the great Dr J E K Aggrey, an African of Gold Coast (Ghanaian) birth. He began by quoting part of the great man's address, "You won't know all about Jesus until the Black-man has brought his contribution as witness to His character. You know that in Revelation we read that 'On His head were many crowns,' and the African will bring his crown to Crown Him Lord of all." The address, for which Arthur wished he had a grasp of shorthand, made a deep impression on the young missionary, not least because, as he said, "The speaker was an African Native, and his audience was a band of about thirty European missionaries – a delightful case of the tables turned."

The fourth element in this enthusiastic report is the question of African education, and it was his awareness of this major theme that was to shape the course of the ensuing years. He wrote that among the "innumerable subjects" discussed, the outstanding one was "Native Education and Government Aid for same". He continued, "It has long since ceased to be a debatable point whether it is right to educate the native, for the native is fast educating himself. The Railways, the Mines, the Plantations, the Stores, the Government Centres, as well as contact with Europeans and educated natives, are all factors in the native's self-education, and these things are here." He compared what was happening in this new territory with the failure in South Africa "for over a hundred years" with the results which that country was experiencing even then. There was hope, he felt, for Northern Rhodesia.

His report closed with a further quote from Aggrey "...declaring emphatically that, educated as he was, it was Christ, not education, had made him what he was..."

The ecumenical stirrings which seem to have begun at the Kafue Conference brought Arthur in 1927 to become Secretary of the General Missionary Conference, a post he held until his death in November 1945. They contributed very largely to the manner in which he then worked and opened him up to become, in due course, Leader of the missionary Team of the United Missions in the Copperbelt. His sense of the importance of education for African people, led him to look for and find instances of what he had spoken about as having "long since ceased to be a debatable point whether it is right to educate the native, for the native is fast educating himself". Coupling that with the outstanding contribution made by Aggrey at the conference, he was sensitised to leadership by African Christians for the church in Africa, and in October 1926 could write in the *Lambaland* magazine, "The phenomenal development of the work at Ndola is the outstanding feature of the year. The secret of its success lies largely in the fact that it is a spontaneous native movement, and the Missionaries' task has been simply to guide it into right channels."

The young Baptist missionary enthusiast, heavily influenced by the style of the pioneer missionary, W A Phillips, was now beginning to develop a new way of missioning, which was both ecumenical and supportive rather than directive of African Christian endeavour. That Missionary Conference at Kafue in 1924 began the growth of the man who was described later thus: "Cross had the gentle strength of the saint. The courage of faith by which he, before all others, had dared to believe in the potentialities of the African congregations on the Copperbelt and to be so self-effacing in his nurture of them, enabled him also, when he felt it necessary, to take an independent stand in deviation from his supporting Mission".[1]

---

1 John V Taylor & Dorothea Lehmann, *Christians of the Copperbelt,* S C M Press, 1961, p40.

CHAPTER SEVEN

Ndola, 1927–1936

When the pioneer missionaries reached and settled at Kafulafuta in 1905, they had first to obtain permission from the government to establish the mission there. They had gone first to Kapopo, where they understood the nearest government official resided, only to find that he had moved his headquarters eighty miles away to Ndola, a village beside a stream of that name, towards which the railway was then being driven to meet Cecil Rhodes's grand design of a Cape to Cairo railway.

Writing in the missionary magazine, *Lambaland*, in 1925, Arthur described it thus,

> "You would approach it by rail from the south. The train would carry you across the steel bridge that spans the Kafuwu Stream (the same that forty miles away joins the Kafulafuta at the Mission Station), and draw up at the loop where stands the white board bearing in large black letters 'Ndola,' with '4076 feet above sea-level' in smaller letters underneath. The station-master's house and office, the Custom House (Ndola being the last station on British territory before the railroad crosses the Congo border), and the huge water-tank complete your view of the station. You would notice the ground rising sharply from the marsh that skirts the stream, and on the

> hillside is the township. Nearest the railway station are the numerous stores serving both Europeans and natives. Leaving the stores, you would pass up the long, shady avenue, flanked on the right by the residences of the Government officials, and on the left by the golf course. At the top is the Boma, or Government offices, with the beloved Union Jack high on the flagstaff in the open space in front. From here a magnificent view is gained of the open country across the stream, stretching away as far as the eye can reach. To the southward lies Bwana Mkubwa Mine 'kopje', and a long straight road stretches from the flagstaff down the hill, across the stream and away up the other side, seeming to lose itself in the thick bush land between. It is down this road we would take you. Just across the wooden bridge we turn off to the right. The path is well used, for it leads to the large native location where live the numerous dusky employees of the stores. A few yards down we come to the school-church, which would be one of the chief objects of your visit."

There follows a description of the building, a brick-built structure with a thatched roof and open windows and doorway, white within, rough plastered outside, standing in a large clearing.

Ndola has long prided itself on being "The Gateway to the Copperbelt", for it was there before the copper was found which gave the area its name, and before the towns which sprang up at the mines were even a gleam in their developers' eyes. The government official who had moved from Kapopo had clearly seen the importance of the place strategically from government point of view. Now that settlement, described so economically above, is a bustling city with its own university, and an important centre of trade and commerce.

From the time of that first encounter with Ndola at five o'clock on a rainy February morning in 1921, the town began to assume a greater importance in the life of both Arthur and Frieda. At first, it was simply the railhead for Kafulafuta, and even on that first occasion, Frieda recorded how she and the others had visited the shops there before setting out for Kafulafuta. While the missionaries at Kafulafuta, under the auspices of the South African Baptist Missionary Society, had served the villages of the rural area round about, people from elsewhere in the then Northern Rhodesia, and from Nyasaland (now Malawi) and elsewhere, were coming to find work in the mines which were then beginning. Only five miles from Ndola was the first of the copper mines at Bwana Mkubwa (and the first to close in the depression of the 'thirties). These "foreign" workers, who were not Lamba people, came with experience of Christianity provided by missions which had long been working in their home areas of Africa. Not wishing to miss out on their weekly gatherings at home, they soon formed small groups who gathered in the compounds, for prayer, Bible study and worship.

We sadly do not have the name of the first of these Christian people from faraway places, but in 1924 "...there came to occupy a temporary position at Ndola a Christian native both able and earnest," wrote Arthur, who, "devoted his spare time to gathering together his like-minded brethren for prayer and praise and exhortation, not only at Ndola, but also at the Bwana Mkubwa Mine five miles away." A small church building was erected at the Mine, but at Ndola "they were content to meet in the open, or in wet weather to crowd into some hospitable native's hut". Very soon they were asking for Communion and, Arthur continues, "on more than one occasion we were able to arrange this." The originator of the church was soon transferred, but his place was taken by others, and this little church grew stronger as time went on, the records showing that there was a steady stream of baptisms recorded, and services had "crowded congregations" with many enquirers being prepared for membership of the church. Help was sought from the Lambaland missionaries at Kafulafuta, and monthly visits are recorded for Communion, baptisms and enquirers. First an evangelist, David "the Ngoni", was released to serve the church at Ndola for a short time, and then he was replaced by a teacher, Robert Mbakaya, a Bemba, who occupied his spare time as evangelist, while being employed full-time to teach in the school which also served as the place of worship. It had been the local magistrate at Ndola who had effected the introduction to the Mission, and he went further by finding government aid to enable the school/church to be built. Arthur records, in April 1926, "three main languages are used regularly in the services, Lamba, Bemba and Nyanja", continuing significantly: "The Church (in every sense a Union Church) has furnished the building with seats (made at Kafulafuta) and provided a good Communion Service at its own expense." The government gave the mission thirty-five acres of land in the Ndola township area close to the "Native Location", and gave "material assistance in erecting thereon a modest rest-house for the use of the visiting missionaries..." To add to the pleasure Arthur had in serving this developing self-governing congregation, the farmer at Chondwe where he and Frieda had celebrated their honeymoon, presented him with a Harley Davidson motorcycle and sidecar "in first rate condition" which enabled him to travel more comfortably and quickly between Kafulafuta and Ndola along the new road then being built.

In a report on the year ending August 1926, we find the following paragraph, in which Arthur compared the work at Ndola with that at Kafulafuta:

> "In reviewing the past year the chief impression is the contrast between the work at Kafulafuta and Ndola. While conditions at the former have, at times, been the most trying and disappointing for years

> (though now happily, the tide is turning), the work at the latter has gone from strength to strength, exceeding all our expectations. It is one of the facts we have to face that after twenty years of missionary work at Kafulafuta, there is little evidence of spontaneity, that this people's characteristic apathy is carried into their religious life, and there is a lack of enthusiasm and a listless contentment with the husks of life, even among those who give evidence of having the root of the matter in them. It gives the missionaries much heart-searching lest that which hinders should in any way originate in them, or in their methods."

Here is evidence of a not unfamiliar experience of those who have more than one area of responsibility, that one part provides joy and the other frustration. Ndola and the mines were clearly providing Arthur with much to enjoy, while there seemed to be a lack of sparkle at Kafulafuta. It is interesting that an unattributed editorial paragraph was added in the *Lambaland* magazine:

> "Friends may be discouraged on reading Mr Cross's remarks about the lack of spontaneity among the Lambas of Kafulafuta, as compared with the enthusiasm evinced by the natives attending the Ndola services. We should, however, bear in mind that for some generations the Lambas, who are a mild and peace-loving people, had been living in a state of continual fear of their more war-like neighbours, and of the frequent slave raids to which they were subject. Need we wonder that the present generation, who begin to enjoy for the first time the blessings of security under the strong and just administration of the British, should be inclined to take life easily. Those at Ndola are not Lambas, and

> most of them come from districts where mission work has been established for two or three generations."

The anonymous writer (presumably W A Phillips, now retired and finding fresh fields and pastures new in Latvia) ends the piece with a text from scripture – "In due time ye shall reap, if ye faint not" – a rebuke to the younger missionary!

Arthur and Frieda moved to Ndola in 1927, on returning from furlough in South Africa, during which the Missionary Society, impressed with the developments there, had approved their transfer.

At first they must have occupied the small "rest house" while the mission house was built, and it was in that tiny place that Myra Anne was born on 30th May, 1927.

Arthur's work now expanded into the rest of the Copperbelt. At Nchanga Mine there was now a similar "union church" to the one in Ndola, where "...a virile Native Christian Community of mine employees carries on the work of God with much success and blessing". This community had built themselves a meeting house and furnished it with forms and a table. They had sent £2 to their friends at Ndola towards the cost of the building there. Here, too, Arthur records, "regular preaching and instruction work is carried on by the natives themselves, and bears fruit". He writes regretfully of not having been able to visit as much as he would have wished, but contemplated monthly visits in the future. There were hopes, too, that visits could soon be made to Nkana and Chambishi mines, and he remarked in his report that "at Nkana the work is likely to receive fresh impetus owing to the transference there of some of the Church leaders from Nchanga". More about this "self-supporting, self-governing native Church" can be read in Taylor and Lehmann's book, *Christians of the Copperbelt,* as, for instance, in the following extract:

> "When eventually this African Church appealed to him for help, Cross, with great wisdom, decided that nothing should be done to undermine either their autonomy or their financial independence. He visited the separate congregations to give advice and to sell books but abrogated to himself no special authority over them, and gave no monetary support. He acted as the local correspondent of the various Missions from which these Africans had come to the mines. Eventually the London Missionary Society, the Scottish Mission and the Plymouth Brethren came to regard Cross and the Union Church as being responsible for their African adherents while they were on the Copperbelt."[2]

There now entered another factor, services for Europeans, and for the first time these are mentioned in a report as having been much appreciated. The earliest of Arthur's sermons in English is one he preached at Ndola in 1928 (and took with him to England on furlough in 1929). The mission site originally "given" though in fact sold for £20 by government was exchanged for another site at the top of Broadway, where eventually there were erected a house for the missionaries, an office and storeroom, and later the Ndola Free Church, where Europeans gathered for worship in English under Arthur's ministry. Sundays for this faithful man of God were long and arduous, often entailing a service in the African church in the morning, followed by services in the hospital and/or prison in the afternoon, and then an evening service at eight p.m. for the English-speaking congregation. The African churches were sending out evangelists into the villages surrounding Ndola, and continued to provide wise and spiritual leadership in the town.

---

2 *Op cit,* p35.

An article in *Lambaland* of April 1929 gives a taste of conditions for the itinerant missionary on the Copperbelt of those days:

> "It was the first long trip in our motor-car...'The old order changeth' – the old order of the caravan of carriers collected for weeks beforehand; the assembling of the necessities, and the too few luxuries, for weeks of bush travel; the arrangement of the loads and the giving attention to a thousand harassing details, and finally the start – inevitably hours after one had planned – and then the tedious twelve to fifteen miles a day behind your line of unknown quantities upon whose heads and upon whose willingness your hopes are carried: this old order is giving way before that of hundreds of miles of well-made roads along which one accomplishes in an hour what used to take a day.
>
> "We [Arthur, together with the Evangelist, Adamson, and an African servant] set out from Ndola on a Saturday morning about 11 o'clock, with a 96 miles trip to be covered before evening.... In the rear...an assortment of articles, varying from motor oil to a week's provisions, from Bibles to blankets, not forgetting the axe and shovel for use on the roads. The fourteen year old car bore up bravely under a full load...and the strain and stress of some exceedingly bad roads. The first forty miles...had been badly holed by heavy mine lorries...to the number of twenty or more a day; a week of heavy rains had not improved the surface. However...we arrived in good time at the Kafue River ferry.... The river is a quarter of a mile wide, and a sturdy pontoon large enough to accommodate two cars or lorries at once takes us across...for the modest sum of one shilling [5p]... [In a few miles Nkana Mine is

> reached] and, leaving it on our left [we] take the fifty-six mile road to Nchanga... . Apart from two stops made in order to clear away trees that had fallen across the road no hitch occurred. Our car attained a speed many younger cars might envy, bringing us into Nchanga at five o'clock."

He then described receiving hospitality in the guest house provided by the mine manager, and making arrangements for the "Service for Europeans" the next day. However, work for the African Christians began at once, necessitated by the fact that there had been no visit for twelve months, during which time there had been disunity among the congregation, which might otherwise have been avoided.

> "Sunday morning the little Church was full of Christians and enquirers who seemed to hang upon the words of one's message – a year had passed since our last service with them – one thinks furiously on such occasions! A second service for enquirers followed, and in the afternoon we observed the ordinance of the Lord's Supper, where the old disunity was forgotten in a renewed sense of oneness with our Lord and with one another. The service for the Europeans held in the Mine Club in the evening was fairly well attended, and appreciation was expressed – it was a year since Nchanga had had a Free Church service."

Monday morning there was a visit to a nearby Lamba village "where there were many enquirers". The story continues with an account of the villagers' pleas for a school:

> "It is one of the hardest things the missionary has to do, than which he would rather face untold physical discomforts or danger, the having to refuse such

> requests on the part of these people, in whose hearts the Spirit of God has implanted a desire for light and truth. But no other reply could be made, distressful both to me and to them, 'We have neither teachers nor money for a school here.' One leaves the village thinking still more furiously!"

That afternoon they were found "speeding along the eighteen miles of first class road" to Chambishi mine where a service was held for the small contingent of Christians from Protestant missions who lived and worked there. Arthur was able to "authorise" one of them to evangelise the nearby Lamba villages. Tuesday took them another eighteen miles to Mufulira Mine, where there was a "vigorous work" started by earnest Christians from the north-east of the territory. Once more, in the evening "after the day's work" they held a service in the open air. "We should have liked to stop a day or two longer," wrote Arthur, "but the 'exigencies of the service' " (a phrase he liked to use) demanded a return to Ndola. So early the next morning they set off back through Chambishi mine and, this time, going to Nkana, "a few hours' comfortable drive" away. In 1922, Arthur had seen two Europeans and a gang of Africans sinking a few prospecting shafts in the neighbourhood, but now there had been a "mighty transformation" with "enormous buildings containing massive machinery springing up". They arrived at midday and by five-thirty p.m. had discovered the African Christians and met with them and "done all that could be done in a short stay". Off they went to be over the pontoon in daylight, between six and six-thirty p.m. or so, which they managed, and then travelled through the darkness of a moonless night back to Ndola. Two mines remained unvisited on this trip. One was Bwana Mkubwa, which was only five miles from Ndola, and so had frequent visits, and the other was Roan Antelope at Luanshya which, being only eleven miles from Kafulafuta mission, also received comparatively many visits from missionaries.

In 1929, Arthur and Frieda, with the two children, Howard and Myra, enjoyed a holiday in England, staying with Arthur's father and sisters in London. On their return to Africa they visited Pretoria, where a new van awaited them to be driven to Ndola for the mission use. The story of that journey is too long to tell here, but is contained in a series of letters written along the route. They camped out at night and had adventures with punctured tyres, but at last Ndola was reached safely. It was October.

CHAPTER EIGHT

The Great Depression and the Opening of Fiwale Hill Mission

That month, October 1929, in far away New York, the Wall Street stock market crashed, ushering in the world-wide financial depression. Missionaries are not well enough off to possess stocks and shares or to engage in trading in them, but Arthur and Frieda were affected very much by the Wall Street crash. The copper mines were, by then, just getting into full production. It had become known through prospecting that the mines were capable of producing 500,000,000 tons of ore, containing 20,000,000 tons of copper. By the end of 1931 the first copper was being exported overseas, but already there was a falling off of demand because of the recession, and the price of copper fell from £72 to £27 per ton. The consequences had been felt locally. The Bwana Mkubwa Mine, without any warning, closed in February 1931. 1,500 African miners were immediately unemployed, as were 300 white miners. The white miners left the area, many destitute and having to be repatriated by government funds, but many of the African miners were redeployed to other mines in the area.

Frieda and Arthur found themselves occupied with trying to help both white and black folk in these circumstances. Strange transactions took place to provide money for white families to travel back to South Africa. For many years the Crosses served their dinner guests from a Wedgwood dinner service that Frieda had bought quite cheaply from a departing family. Arthur acquired a coffin, collateral on a loan of cash, and it was stored in the garage behind the mission house in Ndola for some years. Behind these amusing stories lay deep personal sorrow and pain that the missionaries did their best to try to heal, or at best, address.

One of the heartbreaking stories of that time was of the little white-washed brick church which stood in the mineworkers' compound at Bwana Mkubwa. Arthur recorded the story of its opening and how, before it was built, a hunger was expressed by the residents of the township for some place of worship, on one occasion there being a crowd of about 1,000 gathered into a small space around a magic lantern. A request was made to the mine authorities to allow the erection of a school/church, but it was refused. Not only that, but missionaries were denied admission to the compound. However, the African Christians continued to gather for worship, led by their own people, and they managed to secure "reluctant permission" for the erection of a pole and grass construction, outside which a piece of iron pipe hung for use as a bell to call people to prayer. The management continued to deny permission to erect a more permanent structure, even when the pole and grass hut ceased to be serviceable. After some long time, the worshippers approached the authorities, taking with them their Post Office Savings Bank book, and saying, "Here we have the money, will you please build us a church?" The plea succeeded. On 24th November 1929 the new church building was opened, the £75 cost having been entirely raised by the people themselves. But, as we have already noted, that was within weeks of the Wall Street crash, and a mere fourteen months later the mine closed and the little church became derelict as the people left for other mines or for their home villages.

For Frieda and Arthur the time was not all gloomy, for, on 1st June 1930, their third child, Hugh Geoffrey, was born.

In August that year, the South African Baptist Missionary Society sent a deputation of four to visit the Lambaland field and to assess the work there on completion of twenty-five years work. The visit lasted twelve days, in which time they were conveyed round the Copperbelt and out to Kafulafuta to see for themselves what had been done and what the potential for the future was. As a consequence of their visit they reported back the next month to the Baptist Union Assembly in King Williams' Town, recommending that the mission area be shared with the Scandinavian Independent Baptist Union, who already had missionaries ready to settle there. The Assembly also gave the executive full authority to "re-organise the work in Northern Rhodesia, both as regards mission stations and the missionary staff, with a view to greater efficiency and economy".

A new mission station – Fiwale Hill

In 1931 discussions began in the South African Baptist Missionary Society about opening a new mission station in the east of the area of Lambaland served from Kafulafuta, but the economic climate caused the suggestion to be laid aside. In May 1934, Arthur undertook a cycling trip in the area to "spy out the land", as he put it later in a report. In covering 120 miles he encountered 65 villages, the farthest west being only 15 miles from Kafulafuta, but the bulk of the population resided within 10 or so miles of the railway line, which is between 25 to 30 miles from the old station. The community was a settled one with developing agriculture, including cattle, which until quite recently had not been seen in the area because of disease. He reported that in all that area there was not any school or church "...in spite of the fact that it has been within the Mission's immediate sphere of influence for nearly thirty years".

An ideal position for the proposed new station lay at the foot of a prominent hill, within two miles of the railway, "where there is a piece of high, level land, well away from standing water (this is most important in a malarious country), but within easy reach of a perennial stream...central to the Native population, but at the same time very accessible," he wrote.

In October that year the Missionary Society gave approval for the opening of the new station, and authorised that the headquarters of the mission be transferred from Ndola (where Arthur, the Superintendent, lived) to Fiwale Hill, which the station would be named. The decision did not mean the abandonment of either Kafulafuta or Ndola, but, in line with the earlier decision, the Scandinavian Baptists opened their mission station at Mpongwe, closer to Kafulafuta than Fiwale Hill. The government approved an area of 100 acres twenty miles south of Ndola, centred on Fiwale Hill. Very quickly, the site was being developed, and local villagers had erected a school. As soon as was possible, other buildings including housing for residents and missionaries would be erected.

Arthur now found his workload increased as he tried to maintain care of the united churches in the mines, superintendence of the mission, care of the English-speaking congregations, his work on the Town Council of Ndola, acting as assessor in the court at Ndola, secretaryship of the General Missionary Conference (see Chapter Nine), correspondent with the British-based mission-headquarters in relation to the opening of the United Missions in the Copperbelt (see Chapter Ten), and supervising the opening of this new mission station. The Fiwale Hill project was very dear to his heart, and, immersed as he was in its development, he could not see any good reason to abandon it for any other task asked of him, so that, when the call came to move to leadership of the United Missions Team, he wrestled hard and long with his sense of commitment to the Fiwale Hill project and the thought that in some way he might be honour-bound to complete the task. He even accepted the United Missions post in the belief that, when a suitable leader had been found to replace him, he would be able in a short time to return to

Fiwale. It was a vain hope because the South African Baptist Missionary Society moved to find a successor as superintendent of their mission, and there was no place for Arthur to return to.

CHAPTER NINE

Secretary of the General Missionary Conference

When the General Missionary Conference met in Livingstone in July 1927, Arthur attended to represent the South African Baptist Missionary Society, and was elected secretary and treasurer. Olive Doke later told Howard that the day after Arthur's return from Livingstone she saw him, as she passed the window of his office, doing a handstand or a cartwheel. Intrigued to know what he was up to, she entered and enquired, to which enquiry Arthur reported his election and his elation at being appointed. A rare glimpse of his emotions!

In the accounts of the process of development of Church unity in Zambia, the name of Arthur Cross figures largely in the early years. The story is well told in *Christians of the Copperbelt* and in *Towards Church Union in Zambia.* What was it that Arthur believed and which drove him on in his ecumenical role?

Let us begin with his own words about Christian unity. In 1935, he was asked, as the Secretary of the Northern Rhodesia General Missionary Conference, for his "personal views regarding the co-operation of definitely evangelical missions with the Missionary Conference". He replied as follows:-

> "In the first place I have always regarded Christian co-operation as the mind of Christ. To me it is the Lord's will that we should cultivate friendship with all believers, and particularly so when there is a

further bond, such as the call to missionary service, in addition to common devotion to Christ. Right from the earliest days of my Christian experience I have always had a strong urge to further Christian unity in any way that lies in one's power, so that I have taken up the work of the Missionary Conference with much humble gratitude for the opportunities it presents in this direction.

"The comprehensiveness of the Conference has been misunderstood by many. It has never sought to minimise or ignore the differences which unhappily obtain between Christian communions. All who are in Christ are one in Him. But differences in tradition, outlook, conviction and belief are very real. These differences are, broadly, of two kinds, viz. denominational and doctrinal. In these days the two terms are not by any means interchangeable. Well, I need not argue the value of interdenominational effort to members of an interdenominational mission like the S.A.G.M. [South Africa General Mission, from whom the question came] where Anglicans and Baptists etc work together in unity without losing sight, I take it, of each other's distinctive witness. But the very existence of interdenominational missions indicates that doctrinal differences cut horizontally over many denominations, so that an Anglican and a Baptist (to take an example) may find they have doctrinally more in common than either has with members of his own communion. These doctrinal affinities or differences touch deeply cherished beliefs and we all hold our distinctive witness very dear. This is not only true of evangelicals but also of other Christian people. So that any organisation which overlooks or neglects them is doomed to failure. I believe that our Missionary Conference has had such a long and successful life because it has never set out to compromise any single member's firmly-held beliefs. That is one reason why our membership is on a personal basis, so that personal membership does not necessarily commit the church or mission to which the member belongs. The UMCA [Universities Mission to Central Africa], for instance, with its strong 'catholic' outlook would withdraw tomorrow if there were any suggestions of compromise of its principles by co-operating with, say, evangelical societies. This cannot be said too often. You come to the Conference definitely as a representative of your distinctive denominational or doctrinal standpoint. The more strongly you hold your convictions the more strongly should you feel that your standpoint should be represented in such a Conference as ours. That is my point of view."

The letter to which he was responding had raised a specific instance of the presence of the Roman Catholics and the Seventh Day Adventists. Of the Roman Catholics, he wrote:

"They have never come in very heartily...and only came in at all because it was felt to be useful – a tribute to the effectiveness of the Conference on one wise. They have withdrawn as members. But they still feel that association with the Conference is not to be despised and they wish to be regarded as Associate Members. We take Dr Mott's advice which he gave us last year on this very point, viz. 'Do not close the door to any Christian body. Let nothing in the constitution or name make it difficult for any mission to co-operate. If any withdraw or refuse to come in let it not be for any difficulty created by the Conference itself except in so far as it exists to serve

> Christian co-operation.' That is the Conference's official position. Personally, strongly as I feel regarding the Papistical and sacramental teachings of the R.C. Church I cannot but regard believers in that communion as brethren in Christ, a relationship closer than any earthly bond, and therefore that it is our Lord's will that we should get to understand one another better and if at all possible to co-operate in Christian work."

Of the Seventh Day Adventists he admits to disliking their distinctive tenets as much as he does 'those of Rome', but, he continues:

> "I am bound to recognise in individual Adventists very sincere, evangelically-minded Christians with a real reverence for the written Word of God. And what a point of contact that is! Compare it with contact with purely worldly, religiously indifferent folk all around. And view even these wide differences against the background of heathenism with which we are all in contact day by day. Do not the common points of faith and belief stand out in sharp relief? The same applies to Modernist-Fundamentalist differences, but with this, I think to be added, that these differences are often aggravated by mutual misunderstanding and foolish over-emphasis on either side. This, again, is my own personal point of view purely."

We then catch a glimpse of what Taylor and Lehmann described as "his power to inspire co-operation", and his strong advocacy for co-operation, as he concludes the letter:

> "To my mind the case of such Christian co-operation as the Conference exists to serve is overwhelming.

> And I may add how personally sorry I should be if a definitely evangelical society like yours were to withdraw. I am sure many others would be so too. Those who do manage to attend a Conference usually return home converted! It would be good to see some of you next time, and we trust no untoward events will conspire to prevent your coming."

Well might he have been elated at being elected to serve the General Missionary Conference as its secretary, for the election to that office set the course for a larger task ahead. Up to this point in his career, Arthur had been fulfilling his missionary calling competently enough and to the best of his ability. He had begun nurturing the new African Christian congregations in the copper mining towns, which were to become the Union Church of the Copperbelt, and, as was noted above, he was regarded by some of the mission bodies as their point of contact on the Copperbelt in relation to their members who were active in the Union Church. That was to develop further as he became, by reason of his office in the Missionary Conference, the correspondent with the Missionary Society headquarters in the United Kingdom and in South Africa. That in turn would lead, as we shall see, to his becoming a key player in the ecumenical team which was set up through their efforts, but that comes later in the story.

Secretaryship of the Missionary Conference now brought Arthur into closer collaboration with government through membership of the Native Education Committee and other bodies responsible for development of the country. The Town Council in Ndola gave him a seat as the representative of African interests, not yet having reached the point of electing African people to represent their own.

CHAPTER TEN

Towards a United Mission in the Copperbelt

In July 1931, the General Missionary Conference met in Broken Hill (now Kabwe). More than eighty missionaries were present, among them Arthur, Frieda and Miss Olive Doke, representing the Lambaland Mission. Olive Doke read a paper on the training and instruction of "hearers" or enquirers. Arthur was elected to continue as secretary.

The diversity of matters considered by the conference may be illustrated by two items on the agenda. The first was a matter raised by the Lambaland missionaries respecting the Roan Antelope Mine. The mine had, the previous year, suddenly announced a new rule which said that no services or meetings might be held by the Africans without a European missionary present. The mine claimed that this was to prevent the spread of Watchtower (Jehovah's Witnesses) propaganda. The missionaries protested that this action would be counterproductive. Meanwhile the church was locked for three Sundays out of four, and when groups gathered at the door of the Evangelist's house for prayer and singing they were quickly dispersed by mine security men. Conference appointed a committee to approach the mine authorities, who, seeing the unanimity of the missions on the subject, gave way. Eli Chola was appointed as Evangelist, and before very long a new church building was erected, paid for entirely by the members of that congregation.

The second issue was the broader one of the emergence of industrialisation in the "primitive" society of Central Africa. Already, as we have seen, the Union Churches, spontaneously brought to birth and entirely supported by the African Christians, were already established. Work among the white residents of the towns was slowly coming to birth, but for some time Arthur had been the only Protestant minister available to them, while the Anglican Church provided occasional visits by missioning priests from elsewhere in the territory. There were also some Roman Catholic missions in the area, whose White Father priests gave some oversight to white Catholics. The Rev Dr A M Chirgwin, the General Secretary of the London Missionary Society (LMS), had come out to Northern Rhodesia to visit the LMS missions, and attended the Missionary Conference at Broken Hill. Before he left the UK, he had consulted with officials of the International Missionary Council (IMC) who favoured co-operative mission action on the Copperbelt, and themselves were about to send out a commission led by Mr Merle Davis to review the matter and report back on it. Dr Chirgwin suggested the drafting of a scheme that could be laid before the home mission boards, and eventually a document was produced entitled "A Scheme for Co-operation of Missions in the Copperbelt". It became Arthur's task, as Secretary of the Missionary Conference, to service the committees and working parties which emerged, and to act as correspondent in Northern Rhodesia with the IMC and home mission boards. A fuller account of the developments of this period is contained in *Towards Church Union in Zambia.*

On a personal note, Frieda gave birth on 27th November that year to their fourth child, Rosemary (Romy).

The Team and the Leader

Dr Chirgwin's visit was succeeded by that of a commission sent out under the auspices of the Department of Social and

Industrial Research of the International Missionary Council, under the leadership of Mr J Merle Davis. The "Merle Davis Report" was published in early 1933. Highly praised for its content, there were three major recommendations. The first was that "the missionary work of the Protestant Free Church Societies on the Copperbelt be united under the care of one missionary society". It recognised, however, the importance of the Union Church begun by African Christians and flourishing in all the mines and Ndola, and it believed that this should be encouraged and supported in such a way that the proposed single missionary society should be considered not "as an extension of the Church work of that Society but as a truly inter-church movement". The second recommendation was for the establishment of a Christian Council for the Copperbelt, which would include the Anglican and the Roman Catholic Churches in addition to the "Protestant Free Church" missions. The third was that the YMCA should be invited to be responsible within this framework for the social welfare programme for the mineworkers in the Copperbelt.

By 1933, the LMS was able to appoint and send out the Rev R J B (Mike) Moore and his wife, Joan, to work specifically among the mining communities growing up in the area. This was done as a consequence of the society receiving a gift from "an anonymous donor…for the establishment of new work in Africa and the maintenance of a missionary to carry on that work". Chirgwin, writing to Arthur to advise him of the imminent arrival of Moore, wrote, "The fact that the LMS is entering the Copper Belt does not mean that it wishes to exclude any other society." The hope was that Moore's work would have the backing and good will of the SABMS and other societies. It was suggested that the work should "have the backing of a small Joint Committee with representatives of other Missionary Societies to advise him in his work", as well as the help and support of African ministers and evangelists from other societies. His letter goes on, "I am glad to recall the fact that this scheme is very largely that which you yourself advocated at Broken Hill..." That remark suggests that both Chirgwin and Merle Davis relied on advice which Arthur had given them during their separate visits.

The Methodist Missionary Society was somewhat surprised to learn of Moore's appointment "before consultation with other Societies", and discussions were held in London to try to set things in order. Moore, though, had been appointed in line with the recommendations of the Merle Davis Commission, and "with the fullest consultation at every step...through Edinburgh House" (offices of the IMC). The Methodist representatives had not been present on either occasion when the matter was dealt with. Arthur, on the other hand, responded to the LMS news of Moore's appointment with pleasure. He spoke of consultations with members of the LMS Field Committee, and made the suggestion that Moore should "take up his residence in the Copper Belt as soon as possible, and to this end his stay at Mbereshi (for language study) should be shortened as much as may be considered desirable". He gave as his reasons, first, "the re-opening of the mine at Mufulira and the recent heightened activity at the Roan and Nkana Mines" after the slump of 1931, and secondly, the programme arranged for Moore did not allow him to spend any time on the Copperbelt on his way to Mbereshi. "Let him come as soon as possible and get to work here," he wrote, and after his work had been organised, it was felt it ought not to be difficult to arrange a further spell upcountry. His third reason for welcoming Moore's appointment and wanting him to start work soon was that "My Mission has so much work in other directions on the field and funds are so low that I feel the LMS being able to relieve us of the responsibility for the work at the Roan Antelope and Mufulira Mines is providential".

His other suggestions were that the work at Ndola and Bwana Mkubwa should continue to be the responsibility of his own society, the SABMS, and that "every effort be made to overcome the difficulties in the way of Mr Moore's taking up his residence at Nkana Mine and making that his centre". Nkana was geographically central to the rest of the Copperbelt and was likely to become the largest of the mines, "the building of the Refinery...will give Nkana the largest population, African and European, of any centre in Northern Rhodesia". He ended his recommendations by suggesting that until Moore was able to reside at Nkana he "should make Ndola his headquarters" and he could occupy the smaller mission house there at "a nominal rental". His letter concluded: "I need not say that Mr Moore can count on my co-operation in every possible direction. I look forward to being able to work alongside such a well equipped and devoted worker."

1934 saw more conversations taking place between the mission agencies in Britain, coming firmly to the conclusion that mission work in the industrial situation of the Copperbelt was best done collaboratively, and they committed themselves to support the venture. From 24–27th May that year, a consultation was held in Northern Rhodesia, involving twenty-seven missionaries, representing nearly all the missionary societies at work in the territory, with Dr John R Mott, Chairman of the IMC, who was visiting southern Africa at the time. The result of this was the formation of a committee for consultation as to the best way for the missions to serve the Copperbelt, the chairman of which was Mike Moore, who was by this time beginning to carve out the Mindolo Mission from the bush five miles outside Nkana.

In 1935 came the first strike of African mineworkers, sparked by a sudden rise in poll tax from ten shillings to fifteen shillings (50p to 75p) throughout the Copperbelt. The tax rise was the final grievance in a long list of matters which were disturbing African people, and causing a change of attitude towards the Europeans and the beginning of a distrust which was to continue and grow until independence three decades later. At the meeting of the General Missionary

Conference in June of that year at Ndola, the Rev J G Soulsby, the Conference Chairman, and Superintendent of the Methodist Missionary Society in Northern Rhodesia, made a fiercely critical attack on the government, causing the governor to rush to the conference and make a speech defending government action. The missions succeeded in having changes made in the composition of the Commission of Enquiry into the disturbances, which had been set up by government, with the consequence that its report, published in November that year, was more objective than it might otherwise have been.

The effects of the disturbances and the enquiry were to galvanise the mission agencies into moving more swiftly towards establishing the co-operative work they envisaged for the Copperbelt. The task was to have three prongs, evangelistic, educational, social. Already Mike Moore was in the field fulfilling the evangelism task. A young Church of Scotland missionary, the Rev George Fraser, on his way home on furlough from Mwenzo Mission in the Northern Province, visited the Copperbelt, saw the need and immediately became an ardent advocate of the cause. As he passed through South Africa, he made it his business to call on the Presbyterian Church there to become a partner, and wrung a promise from them of a modest financial contribution to the work. Arrived in the United Kingdom, he passionately presented the claims of the area. His mother, too, a veteran of missionary endeavour in Nyasaland (Malawi), offered to go out to the Copperbelt to engage in work among women for a short term.

On 13th December, a meeting took place at Edinburgh House solely to deal with the Copperbelt. Representatives were present from the Methodist Missionary Society, the Church of Scotland, the London Missionary Society, the Universities Mission to Central Africa, the United Society for Christian Literature, together with officials from the International Missionary Council and the Rev George Fraser. Each of the mission agency representatives reported on the position of their own agency. Fraser made an introductory statement, and then they fell to discussing the future.

Fraser put forward the idea that "the fullest co-operation might be achieved by a group working as a team instead of individuals posted in each mine compound and meeting only as occasion offered". They would live in some central place, such as Mindolo, or at least meet there for "retreats" at which their work would be hammered out, each member of the team having his work allocated to him. "He thought it might be possible to find young unmarried men who would be prepared to go out and take up such work for a few years at the close of their studies.... S uch a group of men could live very cheaply, and if it included members of experience the newcomers could be guarded from many mistakes. Native helpers could be trained at this centre." Such a scheme would also enable the team "to keep in touch with the European communities in the mine compounds". It would be too arduous a task to expect one man to cover work among the African and European communities. The conclusion of the meeting was that each agency should communicate with their missionaries "if possible by air mail" in time for a meeting of the Executive of the Northern Rhodesia Missionary Conference called for January 1936, and a subsequent meeting in London in February.

The Rev T Cocker Brown of the LMS wrote to Mike Moore reporting on the meeting, and sent the notes that had been prepared following it. He wrote, "The following points, I think, were omitted therefrom: – The urgent need for a worker among women...the need, if possible, for people with field experience to be allocated to the Copper Belt: the importance of securing the co-operation of the Dutch Reform [sic] Church and the UMCA."

The difficulties of trying to match decisions and plans in Northern Rhodesia with those being made in London are referred to in the letter from Miss D Gibson of the IMC to Arthur enclosing notes of the meeting of 13th December.

She refers to the forthcoming meetings of the Executive of the General Missionary Conference, and of the Group in London due to meet in February 1936, and continues, "The boards here naturally do not wish to move ahead of the missionaries in the field in this matter, but on the other hand the missionaries cannot very well lay plans or submit proposals unless they have some idea of what backing they can expect from the home boards. We cannot allow this vicious circle however to hold up progress. We hope that the field will be able to give a lead very soon." Hence the decision in London to communicate with the missionaries "by air mail".

Miss Gibson's letter crossed one from Arthur in which he made two important contributions to the discussion, apart from confirming the forthcoming meeting of the Executive in January. "The condition of affairs in the Copper Belt is losing its fluidity," he wrote, "and we must be prompt if we are to prevent things hardening in wrong directions." The urgency of the making of decisions was compelling. He also wrote that, "...it will be many months before I shall move from Ndola to our new rural station, and then I hope to keep in closest touch with Copper Belt affairs." It is clear from this that he had no idea of becoming a member of the proposed team, still less of being chosen as its leader, at that time being heavily engaged in opening up the new mission station at Fiwale Hill for the SABMS.

On 7th and 8th January, 1936, the Executive Committee of the General Missionary Conference met in Broken Hill. The upshot of its deliberations was a series of resolutions "on the Co-operative Approach to the Copper Belt Problems". These were:

1 That our approach to the Copper Belt problems, Evangelistic, Educational (including the Dissemination of Literature), Social and Recreational, should be upon a co-operative basis.

2 That we seek the co-operation of Missionary and other Societies at home in the provision of a team composed both of experienced workers already in the country and new men and women from home.

3 That the Team act under the direction of a carefully-chosen leader, who should be an ordained Minister of one of the co-operating Churches and who has had experience of team work. The appointment to be made by the International Missionary Council in consultation with the local Committee (see 4).

4 That a Committee be appointed by the Executive of the General Missionary Conference...to give general oversight to the work of the Team and to be the link between the team of workers on the one hand and the sub-committee of the International Missionary Council and the different Societies on the other."

A fifth resolution provided for the committee to comprise three members appointed by the executive together with two appointed by the Industrial Labour Advisory Board to represent government and mines respectively, "and at least one African appointed by the Executive of the GMC; with the leader of the Team as ex-officio Chairman". The meeting chose Bishop May, the Rev J G Soulsby and Arthur to form the "Copper Belt Committee".

Subsequent to the executive meeting an addendum was added, approved by "four or five Executive members including the President and Vice-President". The addendum added the Director of Native Education to the Copperbelt Committee, petitioned the governor to appoint the team leader as a member of the Industrial Labour Advisory Board, proposed that the team leader be designated "Director", and proposed that the name for the co-operative venture be "The Copper Belt United General Mission". These proposals arose out of a meeting between Bishop May, the Rev D Maxwell Robertson and the Rev J G Soulsby with the Acting Director of Native Education, Mr J B Clark.

Estimates of personnel and costs were made. In addition to Moore and Fraser, it was perceived that there would need to be a team leader, a trained welfare worker, an "Organising Superintendent for Literature", three women workers, and eighteen African teachers. Additional costs of £4,324, including those of the team leader, £400, would be incurred, against which government grants of £616 and the costs of workers already in the area of £3,000 would be set, leaving £708 to be found. To this was added £500 for "general expenses", making the additional expenditure required £1,208.

The decisions of the executive were duly communicated to all the missionaries in membership with the Missionary Conference, as well as the IMC in London, to government and, in confidence, to the general manager of the Roan Antelope Mine, who had shown considerable sympathy with the proposals. Arthur wrote to the bishop reporting that he had added the addendum to the minutes, and said, inter alia, "I am not sure I like 'Director' better than 'Leader'," but he considered the change of name unimportant. The bishop's response indicates that he, also, was not too happy with the title, "Director", but claimed that at the time they could think of nothing better. "Director" was chosen to enable government officials to accept the office, though "Leader" represented their view of his relationship to the other workers. As far as the mission title was concerned, the bishop said, "United indicates that it is a combined effort of all(?) [sic] the Missions in collaboration. General is intended to suggest (a) the connection with the General Missionary Conference and (b) that our scope is a wide one – not purely evangelistic."

It was clearly understood that there ought to be Roman Catholic participation, partly for its own sake, and partly to encourage government and mines to accept the co-operative nature of the mission. An approach was made by Arthur to the Roman Catholic Mission, but it was not until 1939 that the Catholic Church co-operated in the educational work of the United Mission, along with the Dutch Reformed Church.

Encouraging interviews were conducted with mine officials, and Arthur was able to tell both the bishop and Miss Gibson that they were sympathetic to the scheme, and further, that this could be conveyed to the mine headquarters in London if the IMC chose to approach them.

In February 1936, there were two meetings at the IMC on what is described as "the Copper Belt plan". Miss Gibson wrote that the proposals sent from the Broken Hill meeting of the executive "met with general acceptance, subject to certain comments". These were then set out.

It was proposed that the committee in London should include two representatives from the missionary societies concerned, with representatives of the United Society for Christian Literature, Edinburgh House (the British section of the International Missionary Council), the International Committee on Christian Literature for Africa, "and also, if it can be arranged, of Mining Companies and the Colonial Office".

London was not certain what was in the minds of the Northern Rhodesia folk where the team was concerned. Their mind was that it should consist of those only who were "under the direct supervision of the Committee appointed by the N.R. Executive Committee, and whose time is entirely at the disposal of that Committee", while at the same time having cordial and close relationships with other workers in the field. The idea was of a small group of individuals, European and African, men and women, working in very close fellowship, but "each having his or her own roots in the work of one of the missions in the surrounding country". This could not be the case with the USCL or YMCA personnel, but they could still be full members of the team.

CHAPTER ELEVEN

Arthur Cross becomes Team Leader

The people in London next turned their attention to the matter of the leader. "We thought that there might be some suggestion from you regarding the Leader," wrote Miss Gibson, "but as none came, we took what advice we could get here." They looked for an older man, but he would have to have the gifts "necessary for welding together a group of people of different backgrounds and training into a real team". The possibility had been mooted of the leader being Dr Hubert Livingstone Wilson, then in Scotland and unable for family reasons to return to Africa. Wilson was the son of David Livingstone's surviving sister, and that very fact could obtain entry to places barred to others. He being not available, "...there was no hesitation in the minds of any of our group that Mr Fraser [the Rev George Fraser] was the best person to take the lead". Apart from his experience of team work before leaving Scotland for missionary work in Africa, he also had distinguished family connections well known in Central Africa. Dr Donald and Dr Agnes Fraser, his parents, had served with distinction in Nyasaland [Malawi].

The choice of George Fraser rather than Mike Moore as leader would be a blow to the latter. Moore was, after all, on the spot, had been working on the Copper Belt for some time, and could expect to be considered. Fraser, though considered rather young for the position (twenty-five), had experience of working in teams, and had worked in a rural situation in

Northern Rhodesia. Fraser was present at the meetings in London. Moore was not, and the lot had fallen on Fraser. It was not surprising. It was left to Arthur to break the news to Moore, and to pick up the pieces. He wrote personally to Mike Moore, sending him a copy of Miss Gibson's letter. "I know," he wrote, "that you cannot view this without some feeling of disappointment, particularly in view of your having pioneered the job on the Copperbelt. This was realised at home I am sure. But the choice was left with them, and one knows it must have been a difficult one to make. We can only accept it loyally and be thankful that we have met Fraser and know him to be a man easy to work with and sharing our outlook and ideals." He followed this up with an overnight visit to Mindolo in order to talk through the letter and its implications. Was there a hint in that letter that Arthur had been disappointed, too?

Soulsby's reaction to the letter from London was to opine that "the question of Leader or Director should not be too hastily settled". He felt that it would be advisable to wait to see who were to be the team members first, and then decide on the leadership. While he had great admiration for Fraser, he was not convinced that he had the qualifications for successful leadership, although, "the same was thought of his father in his early days and he became a great leader". Moore, he felt, was "deficient in some essential qualifications for leadership whilst being a valuable man". His letter to Arthur continued, "When the time arrived unless something happened in the interval to upset my judgement it was certainly my intention to put forward your personal claims. I know you are already protesting but that is an additional reason for my judgement."

The Vice-President of the General Missionary Conference, the Rev David Maxwell Robertson, wrote that while they all knew George Fraser well, it might be best if he had the opportunity to spend a few more years "learning his job and gaining the experience necessary for the position of leader".

He had discussed the letter with a colleague, the Revd J S Howie. They jointly felt that the IMC group had not explored the matter sufficiently, and put forward one or two names themselves, including that of the Rev George McLeod, then of Govan, Glasgow, later of Iona Community fame.

Bishop May, Soulsby, and Arthur, the proposed "Copper Belt Committee" in Northern Rhodesia, met on 26th March, with Moore present, and went through the London responses to the executive's previous submission.

They were clear that the London committee should not include representatives of colonial office or mining companies, though they encouraged the committee in London to seek close contact with both. Their argument was that there must not appear to be any going over the heads of local mine managers or colonial government officials, who would themselves be reporting to their London headquarters.

As regards the team, Bishop May was concerned that the phrase "...only those under the direct supervision of the Committee...and whose time is wholly at the disposal of the Committee" would preclude Anglican personnel from participation. However, he said that even if the team were constituted in such a way that the UMCA personnel were excluded, he would still wish to co-operate as far as possible. This led the others to say that the keenness of the bishop to co-operate "should be met by a very cordial effort to adapt the constitution of the team in the direction suggested". There was hesitation about the inclusion of an African as a full member of the team "at present", since there was as yet no one in any way ready for it. "Moreover it is the experience of all missionaries that in order to be of most service to our African people it is necessary sometimes to withdraw from them," they said. They were keen not to be misunderstood on this issue, and affirmed that "the moment there is an African worker who is spiritually and culturally fitted for such close association as is envisaged in the Team it will be acknowledged gladly and readily".

As to the leader, Arthur was asked to write to London "in the frankest possible manner", and he did so in the knowledge that they would "deal very judiciously" with what he wrote. Moore took no part in the conversation at this point, although he was not asked to withdraw. The letter said, "It is with much regret that we find ourselves unable to support your Committee's choice of Mr. Fraser as Leader of the Team." They believed him to be potentially a "most valuable member of the Team", and his previous experience of team work would be invaluable, but "we are not convinced that he is at present a suitable leader". The Broken Hill meeting had had in mind someone older, with definite experience of leadership, and with "proved gifts of personality, able to handle and to evoke the best response from a band of men and women of different ages and experience and religious traditions". Furthermore, their opinion was that in contacts with government and mine officials, the name of Fraser would not mean as much as it did in missionary circles. Even missionaries would take a man "for his own worth only". "A Leader is required who will make decisions and take action on his own responsibility..." and "...authority and experience will be necessary if successful work is to be done".

The local group was unable to suggest names, and had hoped that the wider knowledge of the people in London might produce some. They were even of the opinion that the scheme should be held up "pending the discovery of a suitable Leader than to risk making a mistake in this connection". "Everything depends upon the team Leader. He is the pivotal man in our scheme," they wrote. "The qualifications of age and experience of leadership are so essential that we go so far as to say that actual experience in Northern Rhodesia need not in the last resort be a *sine qua non.*" Nyasaland or South Africa might provide such a person, and if the right man was available, he need not even have African experience. Someone who could give three years to the task might allow the team to evolve its own leader who could quite conceivably be Fraser.

The frustration of trying to have a dialogue by correspondence was expressed in the letter Miss Gibson wrote to acknowledge the local committee's comments. "Couldn't the three of you persuade Mrs Mollison [a famous aviator of the time] to bring you all over here and back again? She could do it inside a week and deposit you each back on your own station again! It is a desperate slow job trying to work out a plan of this kind so far away but if we each know that the other end is sincerely trying to help and not obstruct we shall get there eventually."

The difficulty of discussing the setting up of the team and the choice of the leader through the medium of correspondence is demonstrated by the fact that, after the next meeting of the London group, two letters were written to Arthur. One was from Miss Gibson, and the other from Dr J H Oldham, the General Secretary. Clearly, the local committee's views about leadership and their rejection of Fraser as leader-designate had caused considerable concern. Two issues were raised. One was the nature of leadership, and the other the question of a nominee.

The letter of the 26th March, having spoken of Bishop May's concerns, then quoted him as saying, "any worker who was appointed by the Leader to a definite sphere of work, and was prepared to do that work under his direction and control, and subject to his dismissal, should be a full member of the Team..." This was what concerned London and led Miss Gibson to "wonder whether your idea of a team and its leadership was the same as ours". There should be no question of dismissal or orders, but at the same time the leader should have the power to make his own decisions in harmony with the general policy the team had agreed, when dealing with Mines or Government.

Oldham's letter repeated this and laid heavy emphasis on the way the leader would attempt to represent and express the common mind of the team rather than dictate. "The task of the leader," he wrote, "would be to help to bring about this whole-hearted co-operation and to be its exponent and interpreter." He was even more emphatic in letting it be known on the field that "the possibilities of finding a senior man to act as leader to the team have been explored and have led to no result". He then at length set out to show why the group in London advocated Fraser as the appointee, in spite of his youth, but concluded "we do not wish to press the proposal against the definite judgement of those who are responsible for the undertaking on the spot. Our search for any other suitable leader has been unsuccessful." If, however, those on the spot should be persuaded by the argument in favour of Fraser, please would they convey that by cable.

On 29th April, immediately on receipt of these two communications, Arthur conveyed their contents to Bishop May and Soulsby. Writing to Soulsby he said, "Judging by Dr Oldham's sentence re cabling our decision he evidently expects us to adopt their recommendation of Mr Fraser without further parley… . I have not had time to think the thing over thoroughly. On the one hand we do not want to hold up the scheme unnecessarily. On the other we did not come to our conclusions lightly and we have very sound reasons on our side, closely in touch as we are with the actual conditions here, which we ought not to throw aside lightly." The two weaknesses he saw in their own case were, first, that they had no alternative name to put forward, and secondly, "the fact that in any case London will have a big say in the matter as financial responsibility is theirs, puts us at a disadvantage. It would be a pity if this led us to give way hastily." To Bishop May he wrote, "…one hesitates to question the judgement of people like Dr Oldham…" Clearly London's intention to apply pressure was being felt by those responsible "on the spot", but they had local knowledge and must not surrender too easily.

In the meantime, other members of the London committee were putting their weight behind their choice of

Fraser. Soulsby, writing to Arthur on 30th April, referred to a letter he had received from Methodist Missionary Society headquarters confirming what had been discussed at the London meeting. He had responded, "I do not regret your attachment to Fraser. I have for him great admiration and I am sure he will do a great work in this country. My own alternative would be the appointment of Cross for a short period until Fraser gains a fuller knowledge of the Copper Belt... . I recognise that it may be impossible to secure the release of Cross from his present programme. There is no one else here upon whom I would place the responsibility." In conveying this quote to Arthur, Soulsby continued, "I had previously written in support of your claims for the post: 'I believe he would be big enough to relinquish the post as soon as Fraser was qualified by experience'."

Bishop May also felt the pressure from London. "How complicated and tiresome it all is!" he wrote. He felt London had misunderstood the local committee, and recognised that they were heavily committed to Fraser's appointment. "...In view of the fact that the London Committee regard Fraser as *the* man for the post and *can suggest no one else*, the matter seems to me to settle itself, unless we can suggest an alternative." They should meet.

On 18th May, they met in Broken Hill, and in consequence of their meeting the following cable was despatched to London, "Local Committee recommends Cross leader three years appointment subject Baptist Missions release." It was signed "Bishop May". Soulsby's view had evidently prevailed.

The same day, a letter was sent to the South African Baptist Missionary Society, over the signatures of May and Soulsby, requesting Arthur Cross's secondment to become leader of the Copperbelt Team. They wrote, "It is our unanimous judgement that no man possesses the essential qualifications for this post in such large measure as Mr Cross. His long and intimate association with Native work, at first in the villages of Northern Rhodesia, and subsequently in the Copper Belt, his contact over many years with Government officials and Mine authorities during which he has gained their respect and confidence, his genius for hard, plodding work, his sterling character, his gifts of organisation and leadership revealed during his long term as Secretary of the General Missionary Conference, and his undoubted gift of retaining the confidence of all who work with him – these and other reasons have led to our decision."

That the decision had not been arrived at easily is revealed by their next paragraph. "He is reluctant," they wrote, "to accept this post because of his obligations to your Society and his desire that the special work for which you have commissioned him should not suffer."

They added a postscript to the effect that their decision required confirmation by the committee in London. This was immediate. The London Committee met on 28th May and cabled Arthur, "Committee welcomes you leader." This was followed by a letter from Miss Gibson the next day saying that she had sent the cable to him rather than to either of the others, whose whereabouts were uncertain [because they travelled throughout the country], and she included the important fact that George Fraser and his mother both shared the warmth of the committee's welcome. Writing the same day to Mr Soulsby, she said, "No suggestion of Mr Cross had come from the field and as he was in many ways the obvious man we felt that the omission might be significant. Now that you have made it we accept your judgement without reserve."

Arthur's letter of acceptance, written to Miss Gibson the day after receiving the cable is typical of his modesty.

> "Your cable in reply to the Bishop's message came along yesterday. I am quite unable to comment at any length. You will know by the freedom with which I wrote you in the matter of the Team Leader that I had never thought of myself as a possible leader. I was a member of the local committee and had no

other desire. I asked Mr Soulsby to make this quite clear in his letter to you, as I now know that he had mentioned my name in this connection in some previous correspondence. The Bishop and Mr Soulsby are persuaded that in the initial stages of the Copper Belt scheme I can do some work as leader that there is no one at present quite so well able to do. They know as well as I do that I am not the superlative leader we had hoped to find. I accepted their proposal only on the basis of a three year time limit. The time limit also meets my sense of obligation to my own Society which has just entered upon what for a small society is a considerable extension in this field, and it will make it easier for my people to release me. It is, I am afraid, out of the question to suggest their continuing my salary… . The Society has difficulty in meeting its budget but can only replace me here if they are relieved of the obligation to continue my salary."

Arthur immediately let Mike Moore know what had happened, sending a special messenger over to Mindolo to bear the letter. "We're very glad the home committee welcomes our recommendation. I think it's a bit dirty asking if your Society is continuing the salary grant when the Leader was specially budgeted by us," wrote Moore in reply.

The South African Baptist Missionary Society's response was dated 22nd June. The General Secretary, the Rev Frank Oldrieve, wrote, "We regretfully…came to the conclusion that we ought to release Mr Cross…to become the leader of the Copper Belt team… . Our regret was due to the fact that Mr Cross has proved himself a most efficient and effective missionary and the development of our missionary work in Lambaland is largely due to his initiative and hard work. As a Society we are exceedingly sorry to loose [sic] him, yet we cannot but feel that it is the call of God that has come to him,

Society we are exceedingly sorry to loose [sic] him, yet we cannot but feel that it is the call of God that has come to him, and so we have agreed to release him from his engagement to us as a Missionary Society." The letter confirmed Arthur's letter to Miss Gibson, "I think I ought to say quite definitely," wrote Mr Oldrieve, "that this [contributing to the Copperbelt Mission funding] will be out of the question as we are having to face retrenchment in our work, and of course we are having to replace Mr Cross." That should not lead to the impression that the SABMS was anything other than "keenly interested in all your proposals for the development of this work, and we pray that you may be very clearly guided in all your decisions".

The question of funding the leader now became urgent.

CHAPTER TWELVE

A Miserable Christmas

While all this was happening, the team was being assembled. At Mindolo, Mike Moore was busy erecting houses, church, and other buildings. Dr Agnes Fraser's offer of help had been accepted. George Fraser was the Church of Scotland Foreign Missions Board nominee. The United Society for Christian Literature had found and appointed David Grieg, who, in addition to being well qualified to take care of literature production and distribution, also had experience in welfare work and scouting. The Universities Mission to Central Africa had secured Miss Montague Graham-Harrison for women's work, funded by the Mothers' Union. "Monty" was a qualified and experienced social worker, having worked in London's East End. George Fraser and David Grieg sailed in July 1936 and the women followed in September.

So the United Missions in the Copperbelt (by this time they were using the government spelling) Team was ready to get down to its tremendous task, and all that remained now was to find the money to pay the leader, Arthur Cross.

A letter from Arthur to Miss Gibson, dated 8th August 1936, wrote of the first meeting of the team on the afternoon of 25th July that it had been "a most useful meeting and resulted in the establishment of very happy relationships between the team members. The peculiarity of my own position was recognised but loyally accepted by the others." They had not attempted any decision-making but had discussed or reviewed a variety of matters. The letter then addressed the question of funding the leader. It said,

> "These recent letters of yours have made it evident that the Committee this end and your Committee in London have approached the Copperbelt problems from slightly different viewpoints and that we have been discussing these matters without realising that some of our terms needed clearer definition! This is perhaps inevitable in the circumstances of having to do everything by correspondence. Both the scheme put forward in 1931 and the proposals made in January of this year envisaged a common treasury for everything, including salaries. This has obviously not been accepted by the folks at home – hence the difficulty regarding myself. Mr Soulsby is writing you regarding my salary, etc., but we all feel this end that there are very definite advantages in unified salaries as well as in common discipline...and unified furlough arrangements for all members of the Team. This cuts across the points advanced in the third paragraph of the Memorandum on the constitution of Team etc. which your Committee have agreed to and with the remainder of which we all feel in hearty agreement. Fuller co-operation would be achieved we believe by the adoption of an inclusive budget, however the individual Societies decide to underwrite it."

The Cross family were due for furlough at the Cape late in the year, and it had already been suggested that Arthur, at least, would travel to England during the break so that he could meet the Committee in London and discuss details with them. Miss Gibson was cautious about this latter suggestion which Mr Soulsby had made, especially since "this expenditure would come upon the budget of the Copperbelt Mission Funds". "I do not know," she wrote, "how much would be involved. Mr Cross, I imagine, has no relatives in this country and his expenses would be heavy while he is here.... I think that it would certainly be very valuable for the Societies here to have the opportunity of meeting Mr Cross but I realise that it is going to add pretty considerably to the expenditure necessary."

Arthur was able to reassure her in his letter of 17th June. "Re my proposed furlough in England – my Society will take me to Cape Town. The only expense to the Copperbelt scheme would be my return fare, Tourist, between Cape Town and London. My home is in South London and I would stay with my sisters there.... If your Committee decides to bring me over my wife and family would remain with friends in the Cape."

The matter is not raised again in subsequent correspondence, apart from a letter from the General Secretary of the United Society for Christian Literature, who was acting as treasurer for general funds for the committee in London. In it, he expressed surprise that the SABMS had decided it could not continue to pay Arthur's salary, although it would retain his name on its list of accredited ministers.

By the end of November 1936, Arthur had arrived in England, and had set about contacting the secretaries of the several societies co-operating in the Copperbelt venture.

On Friday, 11th December, the London Committee met to deal with funding, and Arthur attended. Miss Gibson said of it afterwards in a letter to Arthur, "...my brain was suet pudding and I could not get hold of that meeting at all – it sprawled all over the place. I am sorry you saw the more depressed side of the Committee."

Writing to Mike Moore on 17th December, the Rev T Cocker Brown of the London Missionary Society reported, "We had a long meeting of the Committee here on Friday at which our main piece of business was to try and find ways and means of retaining the services of Cross in the Copperbelt 'team'. We explored every possibility, I think, and had reluctantly to abandon one after the other. After I left the meeting, which had been prolonged much over its time, I believe the statement was made to Mr Cross that the inability of the Committee to find the resources necessary for his support must be regarded as final."

Bishop May was in London and should have been there, but was in the Tropical Diseases Hospital having treatment. Arthur wrote to him to tell him what had happened, and his response was, "Your letter fills me with dismay. It is quite disastrous. Of course, if there really is no money to be got, there is nothing more to be said. But I can't believe it." "Have you written to Soulsby?" he asks later, "I don't think he will take it lying down; and it may be that he may devise some financial scheme. He is a genius at it."

One sticking point, for there must have been others, is referred to in Cocker Brown's letter to Mike Moore quoted above. "We had hoped," he wrote, "that the Methodist Mission would be able to appoint an educational missionary who could earn a grant from the Government sufficient to meet the greater part of Mr Cross's salary. The Methodist Mission seems to be unwilling to adopt that course. They feel, I think, that an ordained man is necessary from their point of view because of various ecclesiastical problems that must arise in the development of a United Church. I think, however, that that possibility is not yet ruled out practically." He then suggested that perhaps Moore or Fraser might take up the educational work and so secure the government grant, but recognised that neither would be too happy to change their terms of employment in this way. He continued, "In the meantime, Cross is contemplating a temporary appointment under his church to await developments at the end of the year of probation on which the new missionary is appointed to their Lemba [sic] Mission. I made that suggestion to him...and was glad to find that his mind had already been moving along these lines."

We can only surmise what was going on in Arthur's mind and heart. Here was a powerful test of faith and courage. He no doubt had expected the way to be bumpy, but had he expected the apparent dead end of the meeting of 11th December? Here he was, having been released by the South African Baptist Missionary Society to become team leader of this new united mission, only to find that he was faced with having no job, no finance, and a bleak future, and he had a family to support. It must have been a very bleak Christmas that year that he spent with his sisters and aunt in South London.

Later on, we have an insight into what sustained Arthur at this uncertain and disappointing time. Writing to his elder son, Howard, at the beginning of 1944, he reports on visiting the Methodist Church in Plumstead, a suburb of Cape Town, to conduct the first service of the new year. Howard was in the army preparing to be sent to the Far East, and a long way from home. The letter continues, "I read for a first lesson yesterday a passage I always try to read at the New Year. It is Joshua 1, middle of v.5 to end of v.9. I always remember hearing it on the wireless on New Year's Day, 1937 (when I was in England and the rest of you at Kalk Bay) in the short morning service the BBC puts over. It was a message that was a great help to me then. So I pass it on to you." The passage contains the words, "I will not leave thee, nor forsake thee… . Be strong and of a good courage; be not afraid, neither be thou dismayed: for the Lord thy God is with thee whithersoever thou goest." It is clear from this that these words made a deep and lasting impression on him, and encouraged him to keep on.

After the meeting on that fateful December day, Arthur wrote immediately to Miss Gibson. His letter said:

> "I hope sincerely that you are not concerned on my account at the decision taken by the Committee this afternoon. I am quite happy about my own future,

> wherever it may lie – and on this subject I need say no more. The Cttee's kindly concern and, in the circumstances of their decision, very generous provision for immediate needs of me and mine, is warmly appreciated."

The letter continued:

> "I am very disappointed, however, with the meeting itself – I cannot but think that you too share that sense of disappointment keenly. Time was wasted on matters involving no divergence of opinion but only, perhaps, careful drafting. Large matters of policy were either left untouched or else discussed incidentally – among other things, the budget. More disappointing still, however, was the impression that the key men have not yet realised what a tremendous challenge the whole Copperbelt situation is, and how very badly Missions are going to be let down by any inadequate approach to its problems. If ever there was a call to 'expect great things' and to 'attempt great things'[3] it is in the Copperbelt. Mines and Government are expecting big things of the Missions. I seemed to feel this afternoon that there was no intention to investigate, even, the possibilities of an adequate financial provision for the Copperbelt. The experimental budget of this year and the staffing arrangements already envisaged by seconding men to the work are obviously not to be exceeded on any account. From the point of view of a prudent Mission secretary, a sound position to take

[3] "Expect great things from God; Attempt great things for God" quoted from sermon preached by William Carey, pioneer Baptist missionary, on 31st May, 1792, at the Baptist Association Meeting in Nottingham, from which came about the formation of the Baptist Missionary Society.

up, perhaps. I have felt all along, however, that a great need and a great challenge such as the Copperbelt work presents needs something more than prudence. I am willing to back that up by an 'imprudent' attitude to my own personal affairs. I cannot bring myself, in spite of all that has been said, to accept the decision as irrevocable yet. I have decided not to take any steps as to my future until quite near the time I am due to sail, viz January 8th. After which it would not be fair to delay longer.

"I am not taking up this attitude to force open an issue which responsible people feel has been closed by sheer force of circumstances, but merely because I feel in my bones that there is still more land to be possessed and that all experience points to the reasonableness of expecting 'one effort more' to succeed where a long struggle has failed. Things may happen by a miracle but they don't exactly drop into one's lap!"

Miss Gibson's reply, first describing her brain being "suet pudding" and the meeting having "sprawled all over the place" went on to defend the participants very loyally, saying that they were constantly struggling with tight budgets and making ends meet, and "with that background one cannot be surprised that the vision grows dim at times". "But," she continued, "that is no excuse for a badly handled meeting – for which I feel that some of the blame is mine."

Arthur's response was to write, on 18th December:

"It was really most perverse of you to have taken to yourself personally anything I wrote a week ago – after all the work and heart you have put into Copperbelt affairs! You of all people have nothing to reproach yourself with. Nothing I wrote had yourself in view at all, and anyway I think my little grumble was just a rationalisation of a horrid little feeling I was having that I had let the Copperbelt down somehow. Please forgive me."

How had other members of the team received the news? Mike and Joan Moore were overwhelmed. Mike wrote on 19th December, "Miss Gibson sent me a cable yesterday telling us the terrible news, we really are awfully upset about it. Joan went into Nkana yesterday to do some shopping and she came back with all the Christmas parcels in one hand and this cable in the other, needless to say, the parcels stayed on the floor several hours unopened." George Fraser on 30th December sent a letter to Arthur which began, "I haven't known what to write since hearing from Moore about the London Committee cable. We're all very disturbed and wondering what it means for you and Mrs Cross' plans, and waiting anxiously to get air letters telling us fully about it." We have no record of Frieda's reaction to the news, and the children were not included in the information or its implications, so were unable to share the anxiety.

A meeting of the committee was scheduled for early January 1937, by which time a solution had been found, and Miss Gibson was able to cable Mike Moore, "Cross salary found arriving February", at which Moore despatched a cable to Arthur, "Hallelujah Chorus from the Team".

CHAPTER THIRTEEN

Leading the United Missions Team, 1937–1945

Arthur and the team set off with enthusiasm and high hopes at the start of 1937. The enthusiasm and hopes did not fade with the years, but from the start they were confronted by a task that was not only huge, but beyond the scope of the small team of enthusiasts. Arthur's leadership abilities were under question from the start, but the paradox is that, all the way through, the documents show that it was generally accepted that he was the best person to fulfil the task. In other words, not only did he have a very large work to complete, but he must have been aware throughout that there were doubts about his ability to lead the team. That was hardly an encouraging atmosphere in which to work.

As Arthur left London on 9th January 1937 to return to Northern Rhodesia, he knew that funds had been secured from mission agencies for at least his first year's salary, with the undertaking having been given by Bishop May to seek further funding from "some wealthy men" in England. By 1st February, £100 per year for three years had been promised by each of the mining companies which would cover his annual salary of £300 for that period.

That the team was under constant surveillance is suggested by a report dated June 1937, barely five months after Arthur's return from London. One of the Church of Scotland missionaries at Livingstonia, W C Young, visited Luanshya to see George Fraser's work, and commented in his report to mission headquarters in Edinburgh,

> "The team has not yet found itself owing to lack of leadership. Cross is a keen missionary and a good man but not a leader. Leadership of such a team requires personality, imagination, originality of thought and constructive ability. I do not think the team will be a team so long as Cross is leader."

Nevertheless, the Annual Report of the Team for the year ending August 1937 had this to say about the way the team had organised itself and was working:

> "It is good to be able to affirm at this stage that what (to quote the Draft Constitution) 'cannot be accomplished by statute', viz, the cultivation of the team spirit and the successful integration of diverse views, gifts and capabilities into a unified whole, has been achieved in such measure as to justify the experiment and to guarantee its future success. In any such venture as this, cordial personal relationships have been preserved with an increasing unity of mind and heart. The Team's work has been organised on the principle of allowing each individual member the fullest advantage of each one's particular gifts and qualifications, while making the monthly Team meeting and frequent consultation with one another a unifying and co-ordinating force."

The team leader's task was to enable that "integration of diverse views, gifts, and capabilities into a unified whole". The team had to wrestle over the years with those diverse views, and more than once nearly foundered on different expectations of the end product. There was always tension between those who saw evangelisation as the primary concern of the united mission and those who believed very strongly in the need for developing the educational and welfare work.

The report from the Field Committee to London in August 1938 addressed the difficulties and showed that in spite of earlier misgivings both the leader and the team were making solid progress. The Rev J G Soulsby noted how those who had appointed Arthur had doubted his ability to achieve much, but he was all they had. He continued,

> "He [Arthur] lacks anything in the nature of dazzling brilliance, he is sometimes ultra cautious and plays for time, the word risk is not in his vocabulary, but by his quiet patient and persevering methods he has achieved in a short time more than we ever expected. He has a moral quality which wins the confidence of men and today he is held in high regard by the Provincial Commissioner and the Superintendent of African Education who are at work in the same area. Their predecessors in office would agree with us that any attempt to replace him by any other man in Northern Rhodesia would be a blunder."

High praise indeed! Soulsby then went on to report on Arthur's ability to weld a diverse team into an effective body:

> "His team has been a difficult problem. They are all experienced men [sic] – comparatively eager, independent in judgement and not always ready to accept decisions which have been arrived at after careful discussion. More than once they have set aside such decisions on the plea of principle, thus creating a difficult situation for men who respect loyalty to principle but are careful to differentiate it from prejudice. Mr Cross has handled such a team so well that most of the difficulties in the way of co-

> operation are disappearing and today there is more cohesion and greater loyalty to team spirit and principles than in earlier stages of our work. In this respect there is still room for improvement."

This tendency in the team to rescind earlier decisions on the ground of "principle" continued throughout its life. Even changes of personnel made no difference to this. A letter written in October 1945 by the then Provincial Education Officer (G H Wilson) to Arthur when he was in London on his final visit, received when Arthur was in hospital and which he never read, records angrily that the team had repeated its proclivity to rescindment. He wrote:

> "You may or may not like the decisions made at the meeting. But I am pretty sure you will feel that, having had the opportunity to disagree at the time and having agreed, people should not think it either dignified or sensible to spend a lot of still valuable petrol and possibly valuable time in order to record their disagreement a week or two later.
>
> If the 'Team' had wished to show itself at its worst to the new Director of African Education it could not have done so more effectively. But as you know, this is no more than typical of the sort of thing which you and my predecessors have had to deal with for years now. I do hope you will impress on your people in London the importance of getting some sort of discipline within the team. Government cannot expect the Team always to agree to all Government's proposals. But I think it is right to expect the Team at least to try to agree with itself, to stand by agreements with Government, and to see them actually carried out. And this can be done if someone (I should say you, but that is purely my own opinion

> – and the late Bishop May's, also Opper's and Miller's [Wilson's predecessors]) if someone has real authority within the Team – this is the point I am asking you to press on your people in London."

The kind of authority for which Wilson pleaded was never given, even to Arthur's successors.

Soulsby's report of 1938 went on to lament the fact that the mines had not responded quite as had been hoped, and continued: "Suspicion is slowly dying...we are also agreed that Mr Cross, backed by members of his team, has secured such a measure of goodwill as will facilitate our plans and help our work. Only those who know the Copperbelt as the result of frequent contacts can judge the nature of the difficulties which have had to be overcome, and Mr Cross has met them in fine spirit and with undoubted success."

Among the complexity of difficulties to be overcome were the attentions of earnest missionaries seeking to evangelise in the mining townships. There is a note of frustration in one of Arthur's letters in which, speaking of these good folk, he wrote, "I wish they would leave us alone!" referring to missionaries from rural missions with no knowledge or experience of industrial life making forays onto the Copperbelt for evangelistic missions and creating problems for the UMCB in its relations with the mining companies, who did not or could not distinguish them from the team and the UMCB.

In November 1938, the Rev Paul Sykes, a missionary of the Church of Scotland at Chitambo, in the Northern Province, wrote to Dr Oldham of the International Missionary Council, reporting on a month-long visit he had made to the Copperbelt: "I was much impressed with the enormous amount of quiet, steady effort that has been and is being put into the work. It is a solid effort worthy of respect. Perhaps there is a certain lack of initiative but you've got to remember that the small forces of the United Mission are a few drops in the ocean of work to be tackled and they have so much hay on their forks of a routine nature – education, welfare and their own specific work of evangelisation – that they have not even been able to keep up with the demands made on them, let alone strike out a line for themselves. A larger team is needed and a leader who would command respect both within and without the team. They haven't got the man there and unless someone exceptionally able were to be found it would be unwise to change things. Because of his experience and devotedness, Cross is the right man of those at present there."

Writing to Miss Gibson in the same month, Bishop Alston May spoke about the difficulties and how the team and its leader were meeting them. "...with such knowledge as I possess," he wrote,

> "I consider that he [Arthur Cross] has performed a difficult task with marked ability and a measure of success that to me and others has been quite surprising. He has not had an easy team to handle, and some of them, as well as some of the onlookers, have freely criticised his methods – his caution, lack of push and so on, but his critics have not been amongst those who know their Copperbelt and realise how easily the work might have been wrecked by impatience. Mr Cross has had to steer his course in an uncharted sea through Mine Managers, Compound Managers, Administrative and Education Officers, Beer Hall Committees and the rest, and it is no small achievement, which stands largely to his credit, that the ship should have made so much headway without ever, so far as I am aware, running onto any of the rocks. As I told Mr Cross when we asked him to lead the Team, I did not at the time consider him the ideal man for the job. I thought he was probably lacking in driving force,

> and doubted whether he had the personality for impressing and compelling the big men of the government and the mines. I still do not consider him the ideal man. But it cannot be denied that he has won the respect of the people that matter in a remarkable degree; and I am inclined to think that by his caution and patience, combined with quiet persistence, obvious sincerity and a complete absence of self-assertion, he has succeeded where the 'ideal man' might possibly have failed."

During the course of those years, there were changes of personnel. At an early stage, it was recognised that work among the women of the Copperbelt was a vital ingredient in the United Mission, and women team members were appointed. Dr Agnes Fraser, George Fraser's mother, who had shared in her husband's significant work in Nyasaland was the first. Miss Montague (Monty) Graham-Harrison was the next appointee, having served the Church of England in parish work in London's East End. Monty continued for many years, but Mrs Fraser retired and was replaced by Dr Molly Shannon.

By 1941, Mike Moore sought a transfer to a rural mission station, having reached the point where he no longer felt he could continue in the team with integrity. His was a noble record, and he contributed greatly to the work, but his vision and its fulfilment did not match that of others on the team, so he and his wife, Joan, left, to be replaced by Arthur and Hope Hay. Sadly, Mike Moore was struck down with throat cancer and died soon after leaving the Copperbelt. The Hays had served in China. Their coming did nothing to reduce the difficulties of trying to weld differing personalities and expectations into a unity. The Rev Frank Bedford was posted to the Copperbelt by the Methodist Church, an appointment which caused a minute to be recorded in the team minutes: "That any replacement of staff be appointed as Team

Members, and not to any definite centre as it is essential that the Team have full freedom in arranging the stationing of its members." David Grieg, the United Society for Christian Literature appointee, left in 1943 and became a miner at the Mindola Mine.

A clue to the tensions in the team lies in the fact of its changes in frequency of meetings. At the beginning the team had met monthly. Later this was altered to a day every two months, then to two days every two months, and in 1944 it met quarterly.

Some of the issues refused to go away. In August 1944, the team minutes record a discussion on a report by Arthur Hay and a memo by Arthur Cross, at the end of which it says, "While not agreeing in toto the criticism expressed by Mr Hay, they recognised that these matters had been frequently before the Team in the past and the Team was constantly aware of the need for the preservation of a right balance in its work." Though the papers do not seem to exist, it may be safely assumed that the division was the old one of the rival demands of evangelisation over against education and welfare. The clue for this lies in the team minute of 21st November that year, which records a "long discussion" on immediate and future policy on education.

So much for the internal difficulties of leading such a gifted and diverse team. Arthur played his part fully in the life of the wider community. He continued to be Secretary of the General Missionary Conference, seeing through its work towards the evolvement of the Christian Council of Northern Rhodesia in 1944, and the eventual formation of the United Church of Zambia. He was a member of the government's advisory committee on African education, and on the Film Censorship Board. This latter task involved periodic visits to Nkana cinema to view films to be screened in the Copperbelt beer halls as part of the welfare programme for African mineworkers.

One incident during these years was to stand out for Arthur as significant. In April 1940, there was another general strike of African mineworkers, similar to that in 1935. This time, an ugly incident occurred in a mine township in Nkana in which Arthur and his colleague, David Grieg, were caught up. They had gone on business to the "compound", and encountered an angry crowd of people advancing on the compound offices, which were guarded by armed soldiers. As they moved slowly towards the offices, the car stalled and Arthur was unable to re-start it, so the two missionaries walked through the crowd safely and entered the building. They had barely been admitted when stones began to be thrown and shortly afterwards the soldiers opened fire to disperse the crowd. Arthur and the team were very concerned about the riots and the military action, and were called upon to give evidence to the subsequent government enquiry. The team minutes of 17th April 1940 reveal that the team discussed the "recent events" and decided at their next meeting to discuss the underlying grievances, housing, policing, tribal elders, and it was agreed that in the meantime they would collect the facts about the cost of living of the African mineworkers. The next meeting of the team decided to defer discussion until the Report of the Commission of Enquiry had been published. Armed with these they would have been in a better position to make representations on these issues to both government and mine authorities. The events and their causes are more widely discussed in *Christians in the Copperbelt.*

During the years of his leadership, Arthur's appointment was on the basis of three yearly contracts which partly depended on the availability of funding for the post. It was like the sword of Damocles hanging over the post and the post-holder.

Writing to Howard in October 1942, he said:

> "I have been asked to stay on in the United Missions for a further three years. But I do not think I shall stay on longer than that... . I think I shall feel that the job I came into the UMCB to do will be finished

then. What the future will hold I don't know. But I know there will be guidance when it is needed. There will be some work for me to do somewhere, and so there's no need to worry. The only line of Dante (with perhaps one exception) and the only bit of Italian I'm ever likely to know is 'In la sua voluntade e nostra pace'."

He had quoted the same line, though in English, to Howard some months earlier, and it occurs in later letters. "In his [God's] will is our peace." It suggests what he very much had in mind during the uncertainties of those days.

One of the reasons for Arthur's visit to the UK in September 1945 was to discuss the future of the team and its leader. At this stage, Arthur was minded to press for a contract that would employ him for a further sixteen years. Clearly, he had changed his mind since October 1942. If his suggestion were to be accepted, he would have reached retirement age. The issue was discussed by the team at the end of October 1945, while Arthur was in England and at that stage gravely ill, but they were unaware how serious his illness was.

Apparently the matter was put to them to vote for Arthur remaining as team leader for sixteen years or not at all. That this created a dilemma for members of the team is evident from a copy of a letter from one member to Frieda afterwards. It makes interesting reading for what it says about the team and the tensions. The writer says:

> "Just a note to say how sorry I am that the cablegram to be sent overseas doesn't really reflect the warmth and sincerity and unanimity of the desire to have Mr Cross back as our leader – even in the case of the majority – and certainly the minority would have liked a much longer term suggested in the first instance. It was most unfortunate that the way the question was put before us was the alternative between 16 years and nothing. For no matter how

> satisfied those of us there yesterday were that we had no one in mind except Mr Cross as the right person for our leader, how could we know for how many years those of us making the decision would be a majority of the Team...and we really have no right to decide for our posterity, no matter what we may wish. And another thing I personally thought very significant...there was no mention of anyone else possible [for leader] on Friday, though the discussion was of the frankest. So this...is just to try and assure you how much we do want him back as our leader."

Arthur died before the question of his continuing as leader could be dealt with.

The team and the London Committee were at variance regarding the manner of appointing the leader, and in the end London insisted that the team might nominate, but London would appoint, the successor as leader.

CHAPTER FOURTEEN

The Changing Nature of the Missionary's Task

It is interesting to reflect on how the nature of his work changed in the course of the twenty-four years Arthur served in Northern Rhodesia.

He had offered himself for missionary service partly as a result of listening to the Rev W A Phillips when he had visited Denmark Place Baptist Church and the Cross family home. Phillips would have described the mission, the country, the people, and the task in graphic detail, and it is not difficult to see how the young Arthur was stirred by the images raised of a people living in a remote part of Africa, harried by the slave trade, riven with disease and ignorance, following animist and "heathen" practices. No doubt, too, he had read accounts of David Livingstone's journeys in that part of Africa, and he was not alone in having been stirred by the need of the African people into volunteering to go out to bring the good news of God's love in Jesus Christ to them. The world in those pre- and post-war days was very different from the twenty-first century with its instant communication by radio, television and the worldwide web. The missionary task was a pioneering one in those early years of the twentieth century in that part of Africa.

When Arthur and Frieda landed at Ndola on that February morning in 1921 they expected to follow the pattern of missionary activity of those who had gone ahead of them. To begin with, they had to learn the language. Arthur had begun his tuition while he and Phillips were sailing out to Cape Town. Frieda's language tuition began as soon as she arrived at Kafulafuta. Arthur was expected to study for his ordination exams simultaneously with his language study and while fulfilling a demanding daily pattern of missionary activity. Frieda had already done her theological training in the United States.

An article by Arthur in the October 1921 edition of *Lambaland* missionary magazine gives an account of "daily week-day routine during school term" at Kafulafuta. The day began with prayers in church at seven a.m., followed by work on various manual tasks round the mission. These seem to have consisted of building, thatching, brick-making, timber cutting at the saw-pit, wood work in the carpenter's shop. These were the occupations of the schoolboys under the supervision of teachers and missionary. Others would be working in the citrus-fruit garden, the cassava plantation, or "by our few school-girls who, under the supervision of one of the ladies, have been busily sewing shirts". At eleven o'clock, the bell would sound for another service in the church, from which they would "...file with their native teachers into the various classes..." where they would be taught to learn by heart some of the contents of a simply scripture primer, followed by arithmetic and reading, this latter designed to help them read the scriptures, "the chief end of our educational programme". From twelve-forty-five until three was the lunch break after which there would be more reading and writing lessons before the school day ended. This was the time when the dispensary opened for its second session of the day to deal with a "forlorn group of those whose claims for sympathy, medicine, or both, are investigated by the missionary, who thus completes his threefold character of preacher, teacher and healer". "On Sundays," he wrote, "we are able to evangelise the neighbouring villages by personal visits and by sending native evangelists."

When the school was not in session, the missionaries went out "on trek", travelling either on foot, by bicycle or *machila.* They would visit villages along the way, conducting services, encouraging the school teachers, instructing people who were enquiring about the faith, administering such medicines as they were able, or advising people with sicknesses to travel to the mission for attention. Their days would begin early as people came to their tents to ask for help, and the day would end by a camp fire telling Bible stories with the aid of hand-held pictures or by "magic lantern".

Arthur would also supervise the mission printing press, which turned out small readers, hymn books and other teaching and worship materials. Later on, when he became superintendent of the mission, he would have added to his responsibilities the work of administration including that of handling the mission accounts, including paying the teachers, labourers and other people employed in specific work on the mission station, and later supervising an African book-keeper who would deal with the day-to-day finances.

The move to Ndola in 1927 changed Arthur's working life in some respects, while he still retained other responsibilities. Living in the town at Ndola meant that he no longer had the day-to-day running of the busy mission station to oversee. This was now the task of Miss Olive Doke.

He records long treks out to the outlying villages, such as the trip that began with the seventy-five-mile train journey from Ndola to Nchanga (Chingola). From there, accompanied by an evangelist and another worker, he journeyed by bicycle, covering fifty miles on the first day.

He wrote of that journey that it was "…an exhausting run over rough paths in September heat…" through thick forest, broken at intervals by streams and rivers. "But these vast uninhabited spaces appal one – only three villages did we see the whole way," he wrote. He remarked on the warmth of the welcome afforded them as they came to the villages, and how they held prayer services and attempted to dispense medicines. "An outstanding impression at Sensenta's [village] was of the pitiful need these people have of simple medical attention. The stench of neglected ulcers...obtruded painfully during the services, and Sensenta's wife was preparing for a 200-mile journey to take her twelve-year-old son to Solwezi Government Hospital for treatment."

A letter in *Lambaland* magazine of April 1933 gives some idea of their life in the town.

> "At Ndola here we have the advantages and some of the conveniences of town life – which with a family of four young children are not to be despised. A government day-school helps to solve the problem of education and postpones the day of the missionary's inevitable separation from his children. For him doors of usefulness open on every hand. Apart from the long-established Church work in the Native Location (happily progressing in spite of a drop in population [due to the depression]) and the Reserve work, there is the government native day-school where the missionary gives a Scripture lesson twice a week and generally supervises the scheme of religious instruction given by the Native teachers. At the European School the 'right of entry' is exercised once a week. At the beginning of the year a magnificent hospital was opened in the town a few hundred yards from our house. It has a large Native section, where a skilful, sympathetic Government doctor attracts ailing Natives from far and wide. Here occasional services and the possible opening of a school for the patients call for attention which will be well rewarded. Sunday services in the new gaol, where from fifty to sixty Natives are usually in confinement, are eagerly attended. The work among the Europeans, housed in our convenient

'Free Church Hall', makes encouraging progress while making large demands on our time. It is well worthwhile and has its own indirect influence for good on the Native work."

Sundays, when Arthur was in Ndola, began with a morning service at the white-washed church in the "Native Location" for about 300 people, and would, from time to time, include baptisms in a specially-built outdoor tank, and Communion. After lunch there would be a service at the hospital and then one at the gaol, and the day would end with the "European" service at eight-fifteen p.m. in the "Free Church Hall".

Other Sundays would find Arthur in Nchanga or one of the other mining townships, where the pattern would be very similar, with a morning devoted to worship and teaching for African people and a service later in the evening for "Europeans". A visit to Nchanga would be completed on the Monday with business visits to mining or government officials in the town before returning to Ndola. Periodically, as mission superintendent, Arthur needed to visit Kafulafuta, and on the way he would serve the churches in Luanshya, eleven miles from the mission.

Now, in addition to his mission work, he not only had his work as Secretary of the General Missionary Conference, which became more demanding as decisions were being taken about the formation of the United Missions in the Copperbelt, but he became a member of the Ndola Town Council to represent African interests. His service on the town council was recognised later by the naming of Cross Crescent in Ndola after him. He was asked to be an assessor in the courts to assist the judges when trying cases which concerned African people, and nationally, he was appointed to the government's Native Education Committee, involving committee work and travel to Lusaka and Mazabuka. As we have seen earlier, he was at the same time developing the new mission station at Fiwale Hill, which entailed more of the brick-making, thatching, and other building work necessary to establish a new centre of operations. He fully expected, also, that when Fiwale Hill Mission was ready and he had been able to hand on the burgeoning development of the United Missions in the Copperbelt, he would once again be able to revert to being the traditional rural missionary working out of his new base.

Then came the call to become team leader of the UMCB, which involved moving with the family to Mindolo Mission outside Nkana/Kitwe. The removal meant leaving behind some of the work in which Arthur had been involved in Ndola, such as his leading worship for both the African and European congregations there, visits to the hospital and prison, membership of the town council and his work in the courts. Laying down the superintendency of the Baptist Mission, too, meant that he had to leave the pioneering work at Fiwale Hill to someone else, the visits to Kafulafuta would now be made infrequently and only as a visitor rather than as a vital member of the mission team, and there would no longer be the treks into the bush to visit distant villages. His work ceased to be rural mission and became urban and industrial.

One of the first tasks that awaited Arthur at Mindolo was the practical one of overseeing the building of the house that would become the family home. They moved first into a house, recently built to accommodate the Grieg family of the United Society for Christian Literature, for a few months while the building work took place. Once again, Arthur found himself supervising brick-making, timber cutting, the gathering of thatching grass, and all the intricacies involved in constructing a house and office. This would not have been unfamiliar territory, as we have already seen at Kafulafuta, Ndola and Fiwale Hill.

He also took with him his work for the wider church and the nation in secretaryship of the Missionary Conference and membership of government committees on education and welfare. Similarly, although he had left behind his service to the local churches in Ndola and his religious education teaching in the schools, he found himself once again the pastor of the "European" church in Nkana Free Church (later to become St Margaret's United Church of Zambia). He once again exercised his "right of entry" to the European primary school for a weekly religious education class (to which Myra refers in Chapter Eighteen). He preached regularly in the church at Mindolo and in others of the African congregations in the townships round Nkana. By invitation, he visited the united churches, both African and European, in all the Copperbelt towns to preach and conduct worship.

Although he no longer was required to supervise the day-to-day running of the mission at Mindolo, there were times when he found himself carrying out these duties in the absence of colleagues, as, for example, when Mike and Joan Moore left to go back to rural mission. He was well used to doing the rounds of the printing shop, the carpenters' shop, the gardens, the school, and the various building works which were always a feature of life on a mission station. On these rounds, he would be accompanied usually by the family dog, Spot, and by at least one small boy who found the whole scene always full of fascination and interest.

What was new in the move to Mindolo was his work as the leader of the team. Apart from the monthly day-long meetings of the team, there was much more to do by way of administration. Letters had to be written to London, as well as to government and mines locally. Team members would consult Arthur, and would either travel over to see him, or he would go to their towns. Each team member was required to be a manager of schools, which involved visiting all the African primary schools in the area and monitoring their work on behalf of the government, and Arthur took his share of this work.

A consequential change to Arthur's missionary experience on moving to Ndola from Kafulafuta, and now to Mindolo, was having to learn and speak a new language. At Kafulafuta and in all the villages in Lambaland, including Fiwale Hill,

Wulamba was the language in use, and Arthur was fluent. As the mines opened up and people from many other parts of southern Africa arrived there to work, many languages were encountered among the African mine workers. In the new united churches that they were bringing to birth, services would be conducted in one or more of these. The language used underground and in the mining context between European and African workers was a mongrel, much-despised, language known as "Kitchen Kaffir". It was heartily disliked by African people, and fell into disuse when independence came. It was a language Arthur never stooped to using, considering it insulting to African people as well as a sign of a lazy mind which refused to try to learn an African language. Pretty soon, the *lingua franca* of African people on the Copperbelt was CiBemba, a language spoken widely in the Northern Province of Northern Rhodesia. It had similarities to Wulamba, and Arthur soon learnt it and spoke it fluently both in normal conversation with people and in leading worship and preaching. The country encompassed people speaking five major African languages and over seventy dialects springing from them.

In Ndola, Arthur had served on the town council, but from Mindolo he now was invited to become a member of the Film Censorship Board, which censored all films shown in the African welfare institutions throughout the mines. Prior to the move to Mindolo, Arthur had been regularly in contact with officials of the mining companies in an advisory capacity or to make representations on behalf of the churches and mission agencies. This work intensified with the team leader post, so that he became a regular visitor to the mine offices as well as to the various government offices to fulfil similar functions in their fields of work. Many of these officials, both government and mines, became personal friends, which made contact easier and less formal than might have been the case. In some cases Arthur was not only the representative of the mission to the mine or government, but he would also find himself dealing with people for whom he was also their pastor in the church.

What Arthur now found himself doing was a far cry from the vision he had first had of serving as a Baptist missionary on a rural mission station among primitive and unsophisticated people. On the Copperbelt, he was confronted by all the challenges as well as the problems of a time of rapid development from a rural, pastoral area of Africa into a modern industrial mining community which was worlds away from the tribal disciplines and clear social structures of African society stretching back hundreds of years. He and his colleagues had to help people in and outside the churches to wrestle with the implications of the changes taking place all round them, and to try to come to terms with them. I have no doubt, but I have not the evidence, that Arthur was also in touch with early stirrings of the political nationalism which later led to independence. It is clear that he expected it to develop, and those who followed immediately after him were soon in contact with it and gave it their support.

In looking at Arthur's work over the years of his missionary service, it appears that we have neglected the part played by Frieda, and I ought to try to correct the omission. Frieda had been appointed as a single woman missionary. As we have seen, she arrived on the field having already studied theology and mission in the United States of America. The work of the woman missionary at that time was clearly marked out, and she was expected to be responsible for work among women and girls. If the missionary had medical or other skills and qualifications, these were expected to be put to good use as well. Once she married, she ceased being a separate person on the pay-roll, and became a member of a pair, who were paid as a couple. As we have also seen, the pay for a couple was not very much more than for a single person. So, from the time they married, Frieda had to find tasks she could do which were complementary to those of her husband. She continued to take her part in teaching and leading work among girls and women at Kafulafuta. No longer for her the treks out to the villages, unless she went with Arthur, and that was not always practical nor convenient.

Apart from that Frieda's health was a problem. Before they were married, she had been laid low a great deal with malaria fever, as we have seen, and this reduced her "usefulness" as a missionary. Once the children arrived, Frieda was expected to give up her work outside the home in order to fulfil her duties as wife and mother. This did not preclude her from sharing some experiences with Arthur, as, for instance, fostering tiny orphans until their families could take care of them. The move to Ndola was, for Frieda, a blessed relief on health grounds, although she still had times of illness and needed surgery on more than one occasion for conditions that occurred.

But Ndola opened up for Frieda a whole new area of expertise and busy-ness. Ndola, as has been mentioned, was the rail-head, where missionaries going off to work in the bush would alight and from where they would then engage in the next stage of their journey out. On their way to the coast or on overseas leave, they would return to Ndola to take the train to the Cape. For these missionary travellers, the Cross household in Ndola became their transit camp. Missionaries would arrive heralded by advance letter, or simply "out of the blue", and expect to find beds and baths and meals and conversation, as they always did. This was Frieda's department, and she managed it efficiently and well. The visitors were often interesting and engaging people, who had stories to tell about their lives and missions out in the rural areas. They came from a wide range of missionary societies and agencies. Some were boring, as is only to be expected among human beings. Some were frustrating in their demands and expectations. There was one occasion when Frieda was heard to tell Arthur in exasperated tones about one couple who arrived unannounced and who expected to be given hospitality for a night or two until their train went. While the cook was given instructions to prepare a meal, Frieda set herself the task of making the beds. Her grumble was that "Mrs Mish" had talked without a break throughout this operation while standing idly propping up the doorpost and offering no help at all for the job in hand!

The post of hostess continued to be Frieda's when the family moved to Mindolo. A small "rondavel" (a one-roomed round hut made of brick, with a thatched roof) was built near the house as a guest room, and it very rarely was unused. Missionaries still arrived from the bush or from Ndola needing accommodation for a night or two on their journeys. Team members from the other towns sometimes needed hospitality for a night or two while at Mindolo on business. In addition, there were visits from officials of government or the mission agencies who were welcomed and given the hospitality expected of a mission station in Africa. The mention of mission agencies leads to the memory that for a short stay in Ndola in 1934, the Crosses entertained the veteran and world-renowned ecumenical church leader, Dr John R Mott, representing the International Missionary Council in New York. The author, then a very small boy, recalls the visit of this famous man, principally because he was fascinated by Mott's large, dark eyebrows!

Trying to manage financially as a family was always a struggle for Arthur and Frieda, and not long after their move to Mindolo, Frieda went to work as secretary to the manager of the butchery, the Copperfields Cold Storage Company in Nkana. She remained there until Arthur's death in 1945. She then offered to become minute secretary to the United Missions Team, but this was gently turned down. Frieda moved to Lusaka to a secretarial post in the civil service from which she retired some years later.

Chapter Fifteen

The Fire

In November 1941, there occurred in the Cross household an event that has lived on as being of some significance in the memories of the three members of the family who were there. Parts of the story are reminiscent of the "Keystone Kops" of silent screen fame, as will be seen.

Arthur and Frieda had gone out to dinner with friends in Nkana and then went on to the cinema to see *A Tale of Two Cities*, leaving Myra, Hugh and Rosemary at home under the guard of the night watchman, who was to sleep in the kitchen. During the course of the evening, the watchman's attention was drawn to smoke coming from somewhere high in the roof. It was a thatched roof with a very steep pitch and high in consequence. He then noticed a smouldering patch almost at the peak alongside the chimney over the stove, and realised that the matter was serious. Not knowing the protocols of entering the bedrooms to awaken the sleeping children, the watchman went out to the cook's house in the yard and alerted the cook and his wife. These latter two people led a turbulent married life usually including what would nowadays be described as domestic violence.

On the night in question, cook's wife rushed into the main house, shrieking at the top of her voice, and the three children, assuming that the cook's marriage was once again going through a difficult patch and that his wife was running away from him, tucked their heads under their blankets and affected to be asleep. Very soon they were told the news and all dashed into the kitchen to see what the trouble was. Meanwhile the watchman had run off to report the matter to the other residents on the mission, both the missionaries and the teachers and all the African workers, and soon the place was swarming with people removing furniture and valuables and placing them on what went for a lawn in front of the house. Someone telephoned for the Nkana Mine Fire Brigade and also telephoned to have a message flashed onto the cinema screen calling for the Crosses to return home to deal with the emergency. People appeared from miles around to help or to watch.

Much to their sorrow and frustration the children were quickly taken away to the home of one of the missionaries, so they no longer were able to see this amazing sight.

The mine fire brigade arrived sometime during the evening. It was an open half-ton truck carrying about eighteen fire extinguishers, which eventually proved to be no use at all, since most were not working.

Meanwhile in the cinema the film had reached the moment when Madame Guillotine was busy removing heads from the bodies of the nobility, Madame Defarge was busy knitting beside the guillotine, and there was an air of tension over the scene as over the audience. Suddenly onto the screen came the message, "Will Padre Cross please go out to the foyer," to which some wag piped up in response, "Is he next, then?"

Arthur duly went out to the foyer and was told the news. His friend, C H E Bardell (Bardy, to his friends) had gone out with him to see if there was something he could do. Both expected that it was a call for Arthur to go to the hospital. As soon as he received the news, Arthur left to drive out to Mindolo to take charge of the rescue, asking Bardy to tell Frieda where he had gone, and perhaps to drive her home later.

1 Wedding Day, 16th January 1923. The Rev W A Phillips and some of the wedding guests with the bride and groom.

2 Frieda being carried in a "machila".

3 Bwana Mkubwa copper mine, about 1926.

4 Arthur and Frieda with Howard and Myra in London, 1929, with Arthur's father, Thomas, and his sisters, Winnie and Kath.

5 The family, Mindolo, 1939.

6 The family home at Mindolo, 1938.

7 Frieda and the children with members of United Missions Team (about 1938):

From left to right: *Mike Moore, Mary Grieg and baby Colin, Will and Nell Harrison, Joan Moore, David Grieg, Frieda,*

Shortly afterwards Frieda came out to see where Arthur was. Bardy met her in the foyer, and said, in a very level tone, "Now there's nothing to worry about, Frieda. It's just that your house is on fire!" The effect on Frieda must have been something to witness. Bardy duly drove her out to the mission to join Arthur and the others.

Meanwhile, Arthur, having arrived at the scene, took charge. Men were asked to climb onto the roof and rip out thatch in such a way as to leave a gap between the fire and the unaffected roof, and they stayed along that edge to ensure that no sparks crossed over. Water was in the meantime being brought up from the stream, 300 metres away down the hill, in every conceivable vessel to pour onto the smouldering thatch, and within a few hours all had been made secure and the fire extinguished.

Some of the abiding memories of that night remain...the bowl of eggs perched in the middle of a settee on the lawn...the drunk man who appeared wanting to help and generally getting in the way, only to be felled by a blow to the chin from an exasperated Arthur after the drunk had chased a woman teacher up a tree...but most of all the immense kindness of so many people who turned out to rescue the Cross family and their goods and chattels.

CHAPTER SIXTEEN

In His will is our peace *(Dante)*

By the end of 1944 there was a great need for a review of the working of the UMCB, and it was felt necessary by the London Committee that Arthur, as team leader, should visit London for a series of discussions with the supporting missionary agencies. Travel in wartime was difficult for non-essential journeys made by civilians, but Arthur was encouraged to make enquiries and to obtain the first passage to England available. At first, he hoped to go in January or February 1945, but this proved impossible.

Eventually word came that a passage was available on HM Transport *Mauretania* (a troopship) sailing from Cape Town later in the year. Arthur left home in August, just as the war with Japan was coming to its end, and he arrived in Cape Town "...the day it was announced that Japan had finally accepted the Potsdam Conditions, and there was a certain amount of mild celebrating in the streets..." as he wrote to me from the Andrew Murray Missionary Home in Bellevue Street, Cape Town.

He set sail on Monday, 10th September 1945. During the voyage he wrote postcards to each of his children, as well as letters to Frieda and he wrote a long letter describing the voyage, adding some each day, and posted it on his arrival in England. Because it is so descriptive of the journey and a good example of his style of writing, it is printed as an appendix (see Appendix One). The ship docked in Liverpool on the afternoon of Monday, 24th September, and as soon as he could, Arthur made his way to London, to stay at the family home, by now 30 Poplar Walk, Herne Hill.

The sequence of events from this point becomes somewhat difficult to unravel. It appears that he must already have been showing signs of a cough, which was put down to the damp and dreary weather then prevailing. Various references to his cough or his chill are made in notes to him from people he met during this time. But Arthur was a gallant fighter, and would not allow his own indisposition to interfere with his purpose in being in London more than was necessary.

He attended one meeting of the committee about which Betty Gibson, writing to his sisters after his death, wrote:

> "It seems so tragic that his illness should have come at this moment. We had had a rather unhappy meeting just before Mr Cross took ill – the Chairman was annoyed because there had been a contre temps over an appointment the day before and altogether it was unsatisfactory. Then the next meeting which would have cleared things up was after he was already ill, so that he was left only with the memory of the first and that has been a matter of very deep regret and trouble to me."

Shades here of his 1936 visit and the awful meeting just before Christmas that year. Miss Gibson had wanted to tell Arthur that all was well when she visited him in hospital, but he was "too ill to talk any kind of business". She did, however write to him in hospital:

> "I have always had a very deep admiration for your patience with us at this end of the Copperbelt scheme. The committee had from the outset a fairly definite idea of the kind of man they wanted as

> leader of the Team, but no one has succeeded in finding him. We may have been chasing a Will o' the wisp. You have had a long slow struggle but even outside observers coming home from the Copperbelt testify to your sound building and to the position which the Team now holds in the mining area. The Govt. people I have seen too have spoken in warmest terms of you personally and the work you have done in getting this unique experiment on its feet as a going concern."

She then reported the views of the committee on the leadership of the team, in the future, saying that they were quite clear that they wanted him to continue in that role, but making some variations in the contract.

The "unhappy meeting" of the committee, referred to in Miss Gibson's letter, had taken place in mid-October, but by this time Arthur's illness was beginning to make itself felt. Writing to Frieda on 26th October, his sister, Kathleen said she had been asked by Arthur to write because "he could not bring himself to write to you until he can write more cheerfully, which really means he does not feel well enough". Having been asked by Arthur to write, and in consultation with Winnie and their Aunt Myra, Kathleen decided that they should tell "everything that we know which is much more than Arthur himself knows". She then proceeded to recount the saga from the beginning.

Although he seemed perfectly fit when he arrived in England, he had what he thought was slight indigestion for a few days, then what seemed to be a chill on the liver. On the second Saturday of his stay, he went to a chemist for advice for what seemed a slight haemorrhage of the throat, and when this did not clear up he went to see the family doctor, exactly two weeks after landing in England. The doctor said the bleeding was from a lung and prescribed some medicine "to dry it up", urging him to go for an X-ray; this was taken at St

Thomas's Hospital two days later. The following day he suffered back pains similar to lumbago and remained in his bed or his bedroom, leaving it only to go by hired car to get the X-ray results. These showed no sign of tuberculosis, which he had feared might be the case, but in his elation he failed to realise that the report also said that there was "something on the lung for which examination and observation in hospital was urgently recommended". However, it was anticipated that he would have to wait a further two weeks for a hospital bed, because of the pressure on beds. The doctor was very concerned, but it was not until the day that letter was written, 26th October, that he was able to confirm that Arthur's condition was critical, and advised that Frieda be informed at once.

Arthur was admitted as an emergency case, to the Brompton Hospital for Consumption and Diseases of the Chest on Monday, 29th October. He still thought he was there for tests and would be released within a fortnight. On the Sunday, his cousin, Norman, a farmer in Oxfordshire, and his wife, Biddie, had travelled up to London to see him and delivered three dozen new-laid eggs, a great luxury at a time when they were strictly rationed. So Arthur was able to take the eggs with him, and, as the letter states, "you know how fond Arthur is of eggs".

Arthur's illness had caused a meeting of the Copperbelt committee to be postponed, and he was anxious to get well enough to attend a meeting on a new date. In his weak state he seems not to have been fully aware of how serious his condition was, for he seems to have suggested to Kathleen that he would leave hospital before having the bronchoscopy which had been scheduled for him. That Friday, having seen the GP and extracted from him as full and truthful a picture as she could, Kathleen wrote to Arthur, and although the letter does not actually say his condition was terminal, no one could escape the inference of it. It must have been extremely difficult to write, and to read. One has to ask why she wrote rather than spoke directly, and it seems that in those days hospital visiting was limited to certain days and times in the week. By writing, Kathleen could ensure that Arthur received the letter the following day (they had no first- and second-class post in those days, either, but letters were delivered the next day). Kathleen and Winnie visited on the Sunday afternoon. Of that Sunday afternoon meeting Kathleen wrote later:

> "I had to break the news to him which I did by writing a letter which he received on Saturday Nov 3rd then I saw him on the Sunday for an hour by myself… . We forgot the other occupants of the room (two others) and had a heart to heart talk. He said, 'It's all right, Kath. I have faced it out in the night and I am ready for God's will. I was rebellious yesterday morning and then in the afternoon came your letter and your grapes. Then I began to see what was happening, and now I can say I am ready – but Oh, my poor Frieda, – and the children – I did want to go back to Africa for many more years with them, and to be a better man, – and to do some more work. But I am ready for His will – Oh the words of scripture have been going through my mind all night have been such a comfort."

They prayed together and Arthur derived some comfort from that. At first he asked Kathleen to leave it to Frieda whether or not she came, believing her to be unwell, but later in the week he asked for Frieda to be sent for. He also wanted to see Howard, who needed special leave from the army to go to England.

On Friday, 16th November he was very weak, but gathered together enough strength to discuss with Kathleen in the afternoon his funeral arrangements. Winnie visited in the evening and at his request they did not converse. The next morning the sisters were called at seven-thirty and were at Arthur's bedside at eight-thirty-five, when he was gently breathing but unconscious. At nine a.m. Arthur's breathing ceased, and, in Kathleen's words, "so went to 'sleep' ".

At first Frieda had been unaware of the seriousness of Arthur's illness, but Kathleen's letter, written at the end of October told her the doctor's prognosis and alerted her to what lay ahead. Frieda, naturally, wanted to get to Arthur as quickly as she could, and Miss Gibson had cabled to authorise the fare for her to travel by air to London. However, in those months so soon after the end of hostilities, it was extremely difficult for civilians and non-officials to acquire tickets to travel. The Governor of Northern Rhodesia did what he could to hasten the passage and simultaneously asked the War Office to arrange for Howard to be flown to London from India. Frieda went to Lusaka where she and Myra stayed with the Reverend Edward Nightingale and his wife, Alice, while she waited for a flight. But, for all her best efforts, and those of others in authority, she failed to get to London.

Howard was more fortunate. He was called in by his CO, who ordered him to prepare to embark for England, and the army gave him a priority flight. Even so, he did not arrive until Monday, 19th November, two days after Arthur's death.

Arthur had asked for a simple funeral service to take place in his sisters' home, to be conducted by his cousin and great friend, the Reverend Leslie Clifford Cross, assisted by the Reverend Mr Sabin, and afterwards that his body be cremated and his ashes buried at Mindolo. The service was arranged for Thursday, 22nd November. One of those present was Conrad Opper, formerly Provincial Native Education Officer in Ndola, and a great friend of Arthur's. He wrote to Frieda afterwards to tell her about it. He said:

> "Others at the funeral were a Mr Phillips with long connections with the Lambaland Mission [Charles, brother of W A Phillips], Mr Guthrie and Mr Sabin

> and the two Africans, Chileshe [Safeli] and Nkonde [Brian] who are studying over here, also a Bishop, Maxwell I think, who had known Arthur when he was in the navy [they were shipmates, and Maxwell became a bishop in Hong Kong]. Howard had an arm round each of his aunts – and was very brave. It was a damp dreary morning. I was happy to feel that there were some present who had known your husband in the place where he had worked so well and truly and where his heart rested."

A service was held simultaneously in Lusaka. Later on, memorial services were held in Northern Rhodesia at Mindolo, Ndola and Kafulafuta. And still later Arthur's ashes were interred in a stone cairn in the little cemetery at Mindolo near the house the family had occupied on the hill. After Frieda died, the ashes of both of them were interred in the wall of the church at Mindolo. A plaque was erected in Arthur's memory at the Mufulira Free church, which said of him, in the words of Chaucer: "He was a verray parfit gentil knight."

CHAPTER SEVENTEEN

Letters to his Children

Those were the memories. What of the reality? Rosemary remarked in her letter to me that he did not write often to his children, but that our mother wrote to us weekly when we were away at boarding school. Howard and I kept many of the letters our father wrote to us, and from these there must be some way we can identify better the relationship he had with us.

Whenever my father travelled, he would send us each postcards from different places he visited. The earliest in my collection is a postcard written from London on 10th December, 1936, the day before the disastrous meeting mentioned earlier. The last was written on board HM Transport *Mauretania* on which he was travelling to England for the last time, and posted in Freetown, Sierra Leone.

During a journey he made on behalf of the South African Baptist Missionary Society in February 1944, he sent me a card from Berlin. The name of the place is spelt in capital letters, the date, 10.2.1944, follows. He says, "Dear Hugh, You may be surprised to get a p.c. with the address 'Berlin'. But this is not the city on the Spree, (nor are we on the spree either!) but a small town or village rather about 12 miles from King Williams Town in South Africa." The card continues with information about their destination, and the report that he had seen my Uncle Jack, the younger of my mother's brothers. The references to the name of the town and the river Spree reveal something of his pleasure with puns and plays on words. His sense of humour was so marked that my gift to him on his birthday the following year was a small book of humorous verse, about which, in his "thank you" letter he said, "I am very glad to have it and have enjoyed going through it. We must read a few of the poems together when you come home for the holidays."

When I was sent off to boarding school some five months before my twelfth birthday, I was very homesick. In response to my appeal to be allowed to return home he wrote, "I expect you are finding some things hard to put up with, old chap, but then we all have to come up against these things some time or another. Don't give in. You'll find things easier as time goes on, and if you stick to your guns others will do so too, and I know you will find some good friends.... Remember that very often when we ask to get out of a difficulty God gives us strength to go through it, and that's much finer. So always pray for strength to go on and 'keep on keeping on', and you will get it." On my birthday that year he wrote, "My birthday prayer is that you may be as Timothy was told to be. Look up 2 Timothy 2:1&3." The text says, "Thou therefore, my son, be strong in the grace that is in Christ Jesus. Thou therefore endure hardness as a good soldier of Jesus Christ."

A letter to Howard in February 1941, when he was at Plumtree School in Southern Rhodesia and starting a new school year, encouraged him, as most letters did, to keep fit, and included, "You'll need all your time and all your vim and vigour for what you have set yourself to do. Look up Psalm 71.16 sometime – it's a good motto for you." The verse reads in the Authorised Version of the Bible, "I will go in the strength of the Lord God..." My father was a great encourager, and usually had a text to give or some other apt verse.

As often as he could, he gave me news of our dogs, which were always getting into scrapes of one kind and another. There were reports sometimes of having been to dinner somewhere or of someone coming to stay for a few days. He made no attempt to "dumb down" his letters, as we now say, to meet my age, but rather treated me as an equal to whom he wanted to convey news and loving greetings. At the beginning of 1945, for example, he wrote, "I have not heard from Cape Town yet about a passage to England, so I'm still waiting on. I had to cable Edinburgh House on Saturday to say that I had not been successful in getting off in time to arrive in London by March 7th. I hear that all passenger transport has been in a state of suspension for many weeks. However, now the effort to get off in time for the meeting in March is unnecessary, I'm settling down to the job and will be prepared to go as soon as an opportunity offers."

By this stage in my life, his letters contained appeals to write to my mother more regularly and at greater length – I have never been verbose! One of his last letters to me read, "I know you lead a busy existence and haven't a great deal of time for literary efforts, but it would cheer her up no end if you would write her a little more. We are interested in all you do, although it doesn't seem very interesting to you – all the little, trivial, every-day happenings – they make good material to write about… . Of course, we'd rather have short letters than none at all, so when you are pressed for time, just write the usual line or two, and we'll understand. But I know you will sometimes be able to spread yourself a bit."

A letter written to Howard, aged fifteen and going off to boarding school in Southern Rhodesia, is interesting on several counts. First, it indicates his concern for his children's welfare. It shows, too, a sense of frustration that he was unable to spend more time with us. In dealing with the topics he covers, he respects our own rights to make our own decisions about life. Here is what he says:

> "I wanted to have a chat with you about one or two things before you went off, but we didn't manage to have much time together, did we. You've had lots of 'advice' from one and another and I know you'll

take it. But there are some things that other people can't or don't say that 'Dad' ought to say. I won't write much as I know you don't need much telling! Mummy told me she had said to you that she didn't want you to smoke while you're at school – and it's good advice. When you're older you can choose what you will do – while you're at school it's better left alone. Also any strong drink – I don't think you'll want to take it but some people can be awfully pressing! Never be afraid to say no, or take any notice of being called a sissy. A boy who can stand up and do what he feels he ought to when lots of others want him to do something he doesn't think right, is the man. You know also that we'd rather you didn't play games for money or put money on sweepstakes, etc. It's a bit difficult to see what harm there is in 'a little flutter' now and then – and I admit there isn't much in that. But the principle is worth standing up for."

The letter covers the issue of sex and continues:

"Anyway you know we want you to grow up with a healthy manly interest in all things that are good. Unhealthy interest in sex you will be bound to have come across long before this and you'll see more of it as you go through life. Remember not all boys have a good home training and sometimes boys from religious homes are unfortunately worse than boys from homes where there is little or no religion. So don't listen to 'smutty tales' – no need to be priggish, but a decent fellow just doesn't talk that way or care very much for those who do. And in doing the good thing (the Christian life isn't all 'don'ts'!) you always make it easier for someone else to do it too."

He did not only give advice and offer help, but sought help from his children. Writing to Howard in March, 1939, this paragraph occurs. "I have been asked to stay on as Leader here for a further 3 years at the end of this year – that means up to the end of 1942. It is a big job, and when you pray for your Dad remember he needs much help in what he has to do here!"

Letters to Howard include frequent bits of humour. One is a one-sentence joke, described as "one of the shortest jokes I've heard" – "two fleas retired and bought themselves a dog". Another letter speaks of someone having "gone up country somewhere to join the Air Force as an officer" – it was February 1940 – and in the margin he wrote, "The rumour that he has taken his bag pipes with him to act as an emergency balloon is not confirmed. It's more likely that he has taken them as a weapon of defence." Of course, nowadays he would not get away with that for not being politically correct!

Priorities in my father's letters are interesting, too. On 19th November 1941, he wrote to Howard. His first paragraph said he had ordered some books Howard had asked for. The second paragraph dealt with a railway ticket for the lad's return home for the holidays. Paragraph the third told Howard that his parents would be thinking of him as he sat his very important Cambridge examinations. It included the customary encouragement and the advice to "work – and pray – and you'll get through". Then comes this: "You will see a strange home when you come back for the holidays. We had a fire on Saturday night which destroyed the roof over the kitchen and dining room. Fortunately we were able to save the rest of the house and all our things. We have been very fortunate." He then tells Howard that it will not be possible to re-thatch the house during the rainy season, and that the family would move into the house recently vacated by Mike and Joan Moore, who had left to go to a rural mission station. He left my mother to do the descriptive writing, because he lacked time to deal with it fully. What fascinates me is the "by the way"-ness of his reporting the fire, although I can see how important the earlier matters were.

At the end of 1942, Howard, then aged nineteen, wrote that he intended to join the army when he left school. The idea had been mooted a year earlier and my parents had spoken against it at the time, suggesting that Howard should complete his schooling first, and for that year he was granted exemption by the Director of Man Power, Roy Welensky, with whom my father had discussed the matter. My father wrote to Howard, "Last year we were against it – you were only 18 then and the extra year at school was important. Things are different now. You are older (I had done 6 months' active service at your age in the last war!) and this extra year at school will make it possible for you to take things up again where you left off (should you still wish to do so) when the war is over and you return… . Well, old boy you must make the choice yourself, and may God bless and guide you in it."

One cannot help but compare this with the letter my grandfather had written his son twenty-five years earlier. Grandfather was clearly worried about whether or not my father would survive the conflict, whereas the letter to Howard shows no sign of that terror being present in either my father or my mother. Indeed, it is clear that my father was not a pacifist, and both he and my mother were immensely proud of their elder son going off to play his part in defeating fascism. They wanted Howard to join the Northern Rhodesia Regiment, "without wishing to make the choice for you… . This is the country to which you belong and there are many things to be said for this course of action." Howard was eventually assigned to the East African Artillery, based in Kenya, and was sent overseas to participate in the conflict against Japan.

My father's letters to Howard ask constantly for details of what is happening, but always aware that the censor had to be considered and not offended. They had agreed that when Howard was posted overseas he would find some stratagem for letting them know where he was. They had expected him to be sent to Sri Lanka (then Ceylon), and so it turned out.

However, Howard disguised rather too well his location. Before he left Kenya, where he had been based prior to embarkation, he wrote to my parents telling them that for some time he had been courting a young woman called Celia Longhurst, (Celia Longhurst) and had become engaged to her. My mother wrote "at length" in reply, and shortly afterwards (in July 1944) my father wrote, too. He said my mother would "have told you that we can't remember meeting anyone of the name of Longhurst, but perhaps a later letter from you will help to clear up that difficulty". He then continued with advice to the young man not to rush into things, and so on.

Howard did not actually land in Sri Lanka, but disembarked in India, from where he wrote to tell them who Celia Longhurst was, and my father's letter of 5th August is full of humour at their having been blind to the message. He wrote: "I am sure the name of Miss Celia Longhurst will remain long in our family as a standing joke. How you must have chuckled to yourself at our being taken in so easily! Your powers of mystification put us off the scent completely. Well, we understand it all now, and we must apologise for being so dense."

CHAPTER EIGHTEEN

Arthur Cross through the Eyes of his Children

How does one measure greatness? The writing of this memoir has awakened for the author many memories, and some have slipped in at appropriate points in the story. What has also happened is that I have become aware of the life and work of my father in a new way, which I might not have done, had I not engaged in the research, meagre as it is, demanded by the book.

My father died when I was a little over fifteen years of age, and I am now in my seventieth year. That is a considerable length of time in which to try to bring back into consciousness events and voices of long ago. My brother and sisters have also found the same process difficult.

Howard, the eldest, was a twenty-two-year-old Bombardier in the East African Artillery, serving in India, when my father died. Myra, then aged eighteen, had been living in Ndola working in the hospital as a typist. Rosemary was a fourteen-year-old schoolgirl, about to enter boarding school in Southern Rhodesia (Zimbabwe) to complete her secondary education. It is inevitable that our memories will not coincide on some stories, but also that we each remember different events. In what follows I have tried to piece the memories together to tell the story.

Howard was old enough in 1929 to remember the journey that he and Myra made with our parents from Pretoria to

Ndola in the new motor van which had been bought for the mission. It makes quite a story, recorded in letters to the family in London, with accompanying photographs. Rather than recount the whole story, I will simply quote some of Howard's memories of it. It has to be remembered that travelling by road in Africa in those days lacked the benefits of modern sealed roads and frequent petrol filling stations and repair shops.

He wrote:

> "I remember our first night after leaving Pretoria. We had travelled 50 miles to Warmbaths. Dad must have enquired somewhere and found a level field on the edge of the village near a stream. He emptied the van of all the luggage, boxes, etc which he pushed under the van and around the opening to the underneath along the side he'd used to push the stuff under. It was the dry season presumably, because it wasn't covered with a tarpaulin or anything. He and Mum made up a bed along the seat in the cab, and Myra and I slept there. He unrolled a mattress, spread it in the van on the floor and he and Mum slept there.
>
> "I remember, somewhere en route, after Louis Trichardt, a beautiful area near a river reached by climbing over some mountains, we had a puncture and Dad, knowing we had passed a general dealers, garage and filling station, drove back some 25 – 30 miles to get the puncture (now in the spare) repaired and to buy a new tube also. That may even have happened in Southern Rhodesia between Bulawayo and Victoria Falls."

It did, in Bulawayo. The letter records several punctures, which my father himself tackled and repaired on the journey.

Howard's memories also include the van being loaded onto a train at Victoria Falls to be carried across to Livingstone on the north bank of the Zambesi, because at that stage there was no road bridge as there is now. Howard was again present when the van breathed its last in 1935 on the way from Ndola to the new mission station being opened in the bush at Fiwale. The van caught fire, and our father wrote a graphic account of it for the next edition of the *Lambaland* magazine.

Howard's memories also go back to the early days at Kafulafuta. Like me later at Mindolo, Howard would accompany my father on his rounds of the mission station. He recalls two particular memories. The first was the call to alert people to the fact that the dispensary was open. My father played the cornet, and at the given time he would play a particular call on the cornet, rather like a bugle call. In those days the family possessed an Airedale dog (Pixie), who also went on the rounds, and who used to howl loudly when the cornet call was played, and no-one seems to know whether it was in sympathy or horror at the sound.

The other memory Howard has was of being taken to visit Wa Paul, the leper evangelist. Howard would be quite young, and my father took care to explain that "Paul's hands, feet, legs and even his face, were badly damaged, scarred, etc by leprosy...and that I was not to be afraid, nor express any alarm or horror. Paul's black skin was a patchwork of white and pink areas where the skin had been damaged and the pigmentation changed. Dad also told me that Paul was a wonderful evangelist and he had friends who would take him to nearby villages in a machila, where he would preach the Gospel."

I, too, remember meeting Paul. He was an amazing man who endured his disfigurement and disability with great fortitude, and even put it to good use in his work as an evangelist.

Howard has two other memories it might be worth sharing, for they reveal something of my father's character. One was that on occasions when there were dinner guests at our home (as there frequently were) he would fulfil his duty of carving the meat, but usually he was busy talking at the same time, and on occasions he would stop carving as he became more engrossed in telling his story, to the point where my mother had to remind him sternly to get on with carving. I recall that he was not keen on carving, and once remarked that it might be a good idea if there were dotted lines on the joint to guide the carver!

In a similar vein of forgetfulness, Howard remembers that sometimes my father would drive us children into Nkana to school, taking some work with him, which he would attend to sitting in the Mine Club, of which he was an honorary member. He would also visit members of the European congregation of the town, intending to return to collect us children at one p.m., the end of the school day. However, it was not unusual for him to arrive home having forgotten to stop at the school, where we would be waiting impatiently in the midday heat for our forgetful father!

He also took Religious Knowledge classes in the school. Myra recalls, "I didn't like it when he came to school to do 'Scripture' – I was afraid the teachers might tell him if I was bad!" I remember one occasion when he has handing back written work we had done for homework. As he gave me mine he said, "Cross, it looks as if a spider has fallen into the inkwell and walked all over your page!"

Some of our memories are, unsurprisingly, similar. All of us remember being taken in turn as company for my father on his journeys to Chingola. It was a great privilege to be allowed to go, and it was one way he had of making time for each of us individually. Rosemary, following that theme of my father having time for his children, wrote, "Dad had his office a little way down the hill [from our house at Mindolo] and we would at times go and bother him with our worries, or just to talk to him. What I do remember is that he always had time for us, and would never chase us away and tell us he was too busy. Sometimes he would give us pencil and paper and allow us to draw at a table on the other side of the room from his desk."

Myra remembers, "When I was very young, in Ndola, I hated going to bed because I was afraid I might die, and Dad once quoted to me the chorus,

> 'No, never alone,
> No never alone.
> He promised never to leave me,
> never to leave me alone.' "

She added, "I do wish I had more memories, but the basic feeling was one of security. Mum often used to slap us, but if Dad was angry then it was really serious." That would sum up the feelings of us all about security.

I recall two things about the office being "a little way down the hill", as Rosemary put it. At meal-times we would stand on the house steps and ring a hand bell, and my father would come out and wave to indicate that he had heard, and then shortly afterwards he would make his way home. On a Sunday evening, when he would be due to preach at the service in the "European" church in Kitwe, he would go to the office to make final preparations a couple of hours ahead. My mother would prepare a tray of supper for him, which would include a boiled egg, some bread and butter and a pot of tea, and send it down to the office.

Sundays at Mindolo were different from other days in the week. First there was church to go to on the mission, and often my father was leading the service and/or preaching. We owned a dog, Spot by name, who became a regular attendee at church until the day he decided to prevent other dogs from the mission joining in. I recall a fearful dog fight immediately under the pulpit one morning, and, no one dared to separate the warring dogs. My father came out of the pulpit, grabbed Spot's collar and booted the other dog out. He then took our struggling and angry dog into the pulpit with him, securely held him between his legs and completed the service. Thereafter Spot was forbidden to attend, but the wily animal learnt very quickly the new routine for Sunday mornings and, in order to fulfil his church-going commitment, he would set off early on a Sunday morning and meet us at church!

After lunch, the adults would write letters to their folk in South Africa or London, while we amused ourselves in other ways. Later my father might read some poetry to us, while we took turns in combing his hair. The hair-combing was a favourite of his, and reading poetry or great literature to us while having his hair combed is a memory treasured by the three younger ones. As the day cooled and before darkness fell – it falls quickly in the tropics – our parents would take a walk along the forest road, and we would walk with them. Then, at eight p.m. we would be found in the "European" church where my father would be preaching. I recall nothing of his preaching, but Howard recalls that my mother used to be irritated at a habit my father had of rubbing the lobe of his ear and running his forefinger down the right side of his nose as if he were gently scratching an itch. My mother opined that the congregation would be so fascinated watching these, perhaps nervous, gestures that they would stop listening to, or lose the thread of, the sermon! One wonders if it wasn't she who became fascinated and lost the thread, and it was that which made her irritated!

Not only was my father a keen reader of poetry and other literature, but he was also a keen musician. He had been trained to play the organ as a boy, and he played the piano well, too. Many evenings were filled by my father playing the piano while we all sang songs from *The News Chronicle Song Book.* I still remember him singing "Simon the Cellarer" with gusto – though obviously his teetotal principles were unoffended by the sentiments of the song! Sometimes we would be joined by our friend, Mrs Mary Wilson, who was also a keen piano player, and she and my father would play duets. My mother, too, played the piano well, and so there was much music in our lives. In addition, we possessed a gramophone, on which we played recordings of Bach and Brahms, and often I acted as what later came to be called "disc jockey", winding up the gramophone and changing the records. We were given a recording of Gilbert and Sullivan's *Mikado* which was played until the records were almost worn through, but it introduced us to the comic operas of the duo. My father attempted to teach me to play the piano, but I never did succeed, being unwilling to spend time practising, and neither parent had the time to spend insisting on it being done. My father simply said, "You'll regret it later on," and he was right!

Both Myra and Rosemary remember holidays at Kalk Bay, a suburb of Cape Town, and in particular a pool where we all went swimming, called "Willy's Pool". Myra remembers when my father sat in the sun there and burnt his legs so that "it was very painful for him to walk because his trousers hurt his legs". Rosemary remembers him diving off a tall rock that stood in the pool and was used for diving. I recall learning to swim there, and being taught by him. Those holidays at the Cape every three years were the stuff of happy childhood memories. While we were on holiday there in 1943/44, Myra, aged sixteen, was baptised by our father at Wale Street Baptist Church, Cape Town, where he preached on each occasion that we holidayed at the Cape.

Myra was the butt of much teasing by my father, and they had a very good relationship indeed. Myra remembers one Christmas waking up with spots. "It was measles, I think," she recalls, "and I remember Dad laughing! But I don't remember being offended."

Among Myra's memories, and mine, was the fact that our father kept records of rainfall for the meteorological service, and both of us at different times helped by measuring the rain, as he had taught us to do, and writing down the amount on the records.

For all of us, his death at the early age of forty-seven was traumatic. Howard was given compassionate leave by the army and flown to London, but arrived two days too late to see his father before he died. Myra said, "When I knew he was going to die – I was at Mindolo and I went into the bush and cried my eyes out. But when we got the news – Mum and I were at the Nighties [the Rev Edward and Mrs Alice Nightingale in Lusaka] and I went for a long walk and got a bit lost, but I had faced our loss before that. For some years after that I would wake up crying for him."

Rosemary went to stay with Arthur and Hope Hay, fellow members of the Team at Mindolo, when my mother went to Lusaka, with Myra, to try to fly to England to be with him. "Arthur (Hay) was a horrid tease and I didn't like him," she wrote, "I hero-worshipped Hope who was really very kind to me. When one day I was sitting under a bunch of bamboos in the garden I saw Hope coming to find me, I knew without doubt…that she had come to tell me that Dad had died. She stayed with me for a while but I could not cry and this made me feel guilty because I was really upset. Dad's death was devastating to me and it took me years to get over it."

In my own case, the news of my father's death was broken to me by Eric Fry. Eric and his wife, Edith, had generously invited me to live with them and their son Bill (now Rosemary's husband) and daughter Joan in Bulawayo, Southern Rhodesia (Zimbabwe), while I was attending the Bulawayo Technical School. I shall ever be grateful that it was this wonderfully kind and gentle friend who told me the crushing news of the loss of my father. No one could have done it better, and Eric was a man whom I loved and honoured and trusted, who filled the role of father to me for those three years.

How does one measure greatness? To those of us who knew him, Arthur Cross was a special man. Judging by the letters of condolence my mother received there were very many people who shared that view. There has long been a family story that my father had been recommended for an Honour in the New Year Honours of 1946. Such stories can at best be speculative, but as a family, we have always felt there must have been a grain of truth in it. Arthur himself would not have sought it, and would be pained to think the story even existed! I have not set out to write a biography, for that is a major work requiring more skills than mine to accomplish. I have described this book as a memoir because it depends very heavily on memories of those of us who knew him and on such research as has been possible for me to do. It is my hope that readers of the book may come to know something of the man, and to honour him for what he achieved in his short life.

APPENDIX ONE

Letter to the Family, September 1945

H M Transport Mauretania
Saturday 16th September, 1945

For *the Family – to pass round!*

Dear Mummy, Myra, Hugh and Romy,

Today is our fifth full day at sea, although we have actually been on board this huge ship (there are only 5 larger in the whole world) since last Sunday morning. Once aboard, we were not allowed off, and we actually sailed at 4 o'clock on Monday afternoon. Now we are nearing Freetown, Sierra Leone, which we expect to see tomorrow morning. It is about 3000 miles from the Cape, or just half-way to England. There may be a possibility of posting there, but I may decide to send this by air mail from England as it would then be likely to reach you much sooner. However, I'll start it today and, if I decide to take it on beyond Freetown, I will add to it during the remainder of the voyage.

This is the most steady ship I have ever been to sea in – or am ever likely to be in. Down here in our quarters (known as D3) the illusion of being stationary is real. There is just the slight roll which a harbour swell might give, and this you can often detect only by watching carefully the slow swing of the hammocks. We are about 60 quartered in a "mess deck" five flats down from the main deck, and as this is just, and only just above the water line, the port holes are never opened, so we never see daylight here. We are well before the bridge, just "aft" of the foremast. Here we do not hear the propeller shaft, or the engines, except as a distant rumble, and there is practically no vibration. We are kept fairly well ventilated by forced draught. The size of the compartment is about 30' x 60', and the height of the space between decks is about 8 feet. It is moderately well lit, and one of the lights on a steel support hangs over the table where I am writing, close to where my hammock is slung. I am well used to sleeping in a hammock and have been fairly comfortable. We have two ship's blankets each to supplement any of our own, which since leaving Cape Town we have hardly needed to use. We "crossed the line" yesterday and as the sun is now near the equator, which it reaches on the 21st, we must have crossed the sun only a few hours after. So it has been pretty warm during the last two days and we have not needed blankets at all. Life jackets are now made of some soft material and make excellent pillows, if need be. Fortunately I bought a cushion in Cape Town which I can use on deck also, as "dit is strang verbode" (Romy, please translate!) to take your life belt up there except for "boat drill". For, of course, we do not spend all of our time below. But when we are below we can make ourselves pretty comfortable. There is just about enough room for us if everyone is ordinarily good mannered (as they are) but we should not care to have very many more here. The poor soldiers used to be packed in here 130 at a time! So we're thankful we're only 60!

There is room at night for all hammocks to be slung from the bars provided above the tables, and above the bars there are racks for small articles. On and under the tables there is plenty of room for our luggage, so much so that I went to the baggage room and retrieved my other suitcase, and so have all my things with me – a great convenience in every way.

When troops occupy this mess deck, of course, they eat and sleep in the same place. We are spared that, and we take our meals in a large dining room on the flat above. The food is plain, plentiful and of good quality on the whole, with fresh vegetables, salads, and at least one orange every day. So we have no complaints – indeed everyone is so pleased to have secured a passage that no one thinks of complaining. They are a very decent crowd in D3 too – I have never travelled with an easier lot to get on with, all mutually considerate and pleasant, not an inharmonious incident since we started. There are students bound for English universities, business men of various kinds, one or two officials, a handful of young airforce or military officers being demobilised, and (as Myra would say) a Mish or two to give tone to the party! Among Northern Rhodesians I have met (although some I see only at meal times, as they are not sleeping in our particular quarters) are Mr Diamond of the "Standard" [Trading Company – a store in Kitwe], Mr Wilkinson the Supt. of Police together with Mr Hart, who I think is now a Commissioner of Police, and Mr Palmer the magistrate. So if we misbehave we can be arrested and tried on the spot by our own laws!

Well, of course, we do not stay all the time in our "tween deck" quarters. For civilian passengers practically the whole range of the public decks is open, from the "sports deck" just below the funnels – a very pleasant place – to the "sun deck" just below that, which on other ships is usually called the boat deck, a pleasant place to promenade on; the "promenade deck" below that which is partly enclosed on the seaward side, where large square windows can be opened or shut as desired, and which like the sun deck above, goes completely round the cabin accommodation. Both towards the fo'c'sle and the stern there are wide open decks also where one may walk. So walking about the ship is interesting and provides good exercise.

Of course all this space is needed. There are 5000 people travelling (apart from the crew and ship's staff who number some hundreds) and so the decks are pretty crowded during all waking hours, and at night the men are allowed to sleep on deck in certain parts until 6 a.m. when the deck parties start to wash down.

Twice we have had "boat drill", when everybody musters at their particular emergency station, wearing lifebelts. Then it is you see something of the numbers travelling. The ship resembles a grand-stand at a cup-final, and there's hardly an inch of deck to be seen!

There are few signs left of the luxurious fittings the ship must have had in peace-time. The lighting and panelling of the large dining room and lounges, theatre, &c. of what used to be the First Class portion are an indication of the former splendour. Men and women are separated, even where families are travelling, so that a maximum number of berths are occupied. There are a large number of children on board, most of them evacuees going home 3, 4 & 5 years older than they were when they came away. The girls are scattered about among the women's cabins. The boys occupy bunks in what used to be the steerage quarters, right aft. The majority of the servicemen travelling are R.A.F's, and a very quiet, well-behaved crowd they are.

Thursday 20th September

I had reached the above point when we came in sight of Freetown, and I decided to write a post card to you all and give them to a friend who was amongst the 4 passengers who were disembarking there, and to ask him to post them for me – that to Mummy (in an envelope with a few other papers) by air mail, the rest by surface. So it is extremely likely that you will get this letter first. I'm sorry I couldn't get picture postcards. My first knowledge of the existence of such a place as Freetown I got when about 9 years old from a picture p.c. posted there by a "mish" (Myra will explain what this is) who was on his way to the Congo. So it was a bit of a thrill for me to have the opportunity of seeing the place, if only from a mile off shore. The reason picture p.c.s were unobtainable was that the ship's commander forbade very strictly any trading with the "bumboats", as they are called, in which natives displayed fruit and other things for sale. The reason behind the order was that the cleanliness of the articles was doubtful and sickness, and even epidemics on such a crowded ship as ours, might be introduced. The usual diving for sixpences took place, of course.

Most of the boats were just dug-out canoes, like the Northern Rhodesian article, but, I think, made from much lighter, softer trees than ours, and most were painted red or green, inside and out. Usually there were two people, one to paddle the canoe, the other to dive for the money. But here and there was the independent man who paddled his own canoe and did his own diving. The paddles had much broader blades than our natives' make, and were also painted, making them look like broad-bladed spears. And they were painted in various gay colours. In spite of the Commander's orders – which were strictly obeyed by the troops and civilian passengers, the crew of our ship, secure in their jobs these days, did trade with the boats, leading to an amusing incident which I'll relate later.

Sierra Leone is reputedly a beautiful place (to look at, at least – like some ladies, Myra, before you get to know them!) I didn't know, or had forgotten if I ever knew, that Freetown is on the south bank of the estuary of a considerable river – called, I believe, the Sierra Leone river – which at that point (6 miles from the mouth) is about 5 miles wide. If any of you know this you can have full marks for it! Freetown straggles along a strip of coast line like that between Muizenberg and Fish Hoek, only you must imagine it a little wider, and the mountains to be not quite as high, and not rugged at all. There are no bluffs – the S.L. Mountains are more like large rounded hills, covered with luxuriant vegetation from foot to summit. Obviously everything grows lush there, palm trees occur frequently, and everything was very green. Your Typical Tropical Scene, in fact. The houses are mostly small, as the bulk of the population is Negro. This stretch of coast once bore the only too well deserved name of The White Man's Grave. One can well believe it. One of the chief products of the country is Malaria, and it used even to be noted for one of the best Yellow Fever ports in the world. Health conditions are, undoubtedly greatly improved now, but the "O.C. Troops" (whose orders we are all under onboard) forbade anyone to take their hammocks on deck during the one night we lay anchored off the port, as a precaution against Malaria – a mile, apparently, being nothing to the stout mosquitoes they breed there! I must say I offered up a prayer of thankfulness that my sphere of work did not lie in Sierra Leone. As you will gather from my post cards, the weather was decidedly hot – a steamy, damp heat, of the kind that we are mercifully spared from as a rule in N.R. Between decks that night was, for me at any rate, simply unbearable, and from 3 a.m. I wandered about the ship's upper decks where it was, in comparison, beautifully cool. There was no order against walking about! I'm told that in the cabins – including the First Class – things were as bad, and few people slept that night. It has to be remembered that the Mauretania was designed and built for the Transatlantic run, where even in summer the shipping routes go far enough north for the weather to be cold most of the time (ask Mummy to confirm this – she has done it) and consequently we felt it more than we should have in a Union Castle boat.

Next morning we looked out to see a great wet cloud settling down on the mountains on shore, and soon after breakfast down came the rain in sheets. It rained without intermission all the morning, driving everybody under cover, making the decks run with water, and beating in at every opening. The Ship's Pessimist, who you will find on all ships, asked if we had heard that we should have to lie off Freetown for three or four days at least. We hadn't. Some people informed him so in livid language. How the fellow escaped being pitched out into rain and sea for the sword fish (which they keep here instead of sharks) to tickle, is a mystery. Fortunately the refuelling (we emptied 2 whole tanks!) and fresh watering, were completed soon after mid-day and lank, damp, and lugubrious faces all over the ship brightened when they heard the hauling on the anchor cable and saw the hauling down of the black ball on the forestay, signifying that the anchor was clear. In a few minutes we were gliding out of the Sierra Leone river, five thousand people registering firm determination never to see the place again if they could help it! Now the amusing incident: One of the canoes had sent a basket up to one of the port holes in the crew's quarters in the fo'c'sle – selling bananas probably. The anchor was up and the great ship under way before the transaction was completed, and the wicked sailormen hung on to the basket which was still attached to a cord in the hand of its owner in the canoe, who besought them piteously to let it go. He held on to it as long as he could, the consequence being that the Mauretania, towering like a mountain over the canoe began to tow the canoe rapidly through the water at an alarming speed for its occupants – and it's astonishing how quickly these enormous ships gather speed when once under way. Of course they had to let go at last to avoid being swamped, and, I am glad to say, the bad sailormen then threw the basket well out where its owner could recover it. We should have hated to see the incident carried further than that. And we all hoped the bananas had been paid for.

Well, we were soon headed north, and it was remarkable how the cool head wind (which we expected to encounter north of the Line) put everyone into a thoroughly good humour. How briskly they all walked round the promenade decks and how wonderfully tolerant everyone was of the faces and idiosyncrasies of people who in the damp heat they would have cheerfully thrown overboard, had it not been that the throwing of litter over the ship's side is strictly forbidden.

Even the Ship's Pessimist looked a little less careworn than usual.

Since then the weather has been getting steadily cooler. Up to this morning speculation had been rife as to where exactly we should be landed in England. At Freetown we were told, officially, that, weather permitting, we should arrive on Sunday 23rd, but that the port to be made for would not be known for some days. Southampton or Liverpool (the ship's home port) seemed to be the two reasonable alternatives. The Ship's Pessimist asked if we had heard that it would be the Clyde, after all, and that not till Wednesday week. A smile wreathed the face of the only Scotsman we have with us in D3, but the rest only groaned and said, with strained politeness but some emphasis, No, we hadn't. "Because", went on the S.P. "it would be stark tragedy for most of us". He ought really to ask the steward to taste every cup of coffee he drinks, for I'm sure someone will put a pinch of white powder in it for him one day. Actually the odds are pretty even. Those whose homes and business is in the north of England wished for Liverpool —the rest for S'hampton.

This morning, over the "blower" (as they call the loud speaker system by which orders, news &c is broadcast throughout the ship) came a voice saying, "This is the Master. I have had orders from the Admiralty this morning to take this ship to Liverpool, and, weather permitting, we should be alongside the landing stage in the afternoon or evening of Sunday. That is all." Well, I am not really sorry. I shall see two things I have wanted to see for many years – Liverpool Cathedral (where I should like to think I could attend Evensong on Sunday) and the Mersey Tunnel. Also I shall see something of the north of England which is so much a foreign land to us southern Englishmen.

Saturday 22nd September

I had reached thus far when we had to vacate the "mess deck" for the morning inspection by O.C. Troops, and I didn't get down to writing again that day. Yesterday we ran into quite a heavy swell, having left the coast of Africa and begun to sail west of Portugal towards "the Bay" which we went through during the afternoon and night. For the first time we have felt we were really at sea, although the mighty heavings of this colossal ship are unlike anything else I have experienced – very slow and very majestic. "Who mentioned heavings"? moaned the S.P. – and promptly disappeared on his own private business! Actually it has taken very few people that way, but it has caused a series of headaches and some tummy upsets. The only effect on me was a bit of a headache yesterday morning, which yielded to a couple of Aspirin tablets. Well, the swell is still on, and it is a cold day with mist and rain. I hardly think we're out of the Bay yet, but there's no knowing. The day's runs are not posted up as they are in a Union Castle boat, so we're left to our guesses, based upon the time the skipper expects to reach Liverpool. There are few or no landmarks, of course. The last one was the island of Madeira which we passed about 5 or 6 miles to the west of us two mornings ago. But as we get near the shores of England we expect to see at least a light or two at nights. Anyway the weather isn't holding us up, so in spite of S.P. No 2, whom I heard saying this morning, "We can't arrive until Monday – anyway who wants to!" most of us hope we shall see Liverpool tomorrow afternoon. I shan't be able to write much after today so I'll finish off and leave the envelope open for a few last words before posting it, as I hope, in Liverpool.

Now about a few shipboard friendships. A group of about 18 fellows, RAFs mostly with one or two naval and army men, have been meeting daily for Bible study and prayer, and again for a "free and easy" service in the ship's library in the evening. We have had some good times together. The leading spirits have been a PB major named Sheward, a man I admire more for his character (sterling) than his judgement!; a "Heart of Africa" (Studd's mission) "mish", who left us at Freetown, who was an Australian and a real live wire; two PB missionaries who were at the Andrew Murray Home, bachelor brothers named Mock from the Congo; and for the rest the young fellows – like Lawrie Warburton (Sergt. R A F) going in for the C of E Ministry, Frank Robinson (civilian and only 18 – going to Manchester University also to train for the C of E ministry (only the opposite end from Laurie, who is Evangelical while Frank is highest of high A C), and Les de Smidt, Baptist (engaged to Agnes Mathew, daughter of the Wynberg Mathew who is in England now). Les is going home to train for the British Syrian Mission, having felt the call to that work while in Syria during the war as a surveyor in the UDF. Good lad, Les. Others include a Baptist or two, one Salvation Army lad who intends training as an officer, a Methodist or two and one or two more PBs. As I say, we have had some good times. The PBs have not had it all their own way! But there has been a very happy spirit of fellowship among us, and we shall be sorry to part company with one another. The meetings have certainly lit up an otherwise rather dull voyage, and I am sure have done us all good. They have done me good, at least, and the contacts have been good.

My particular friend has been Frank Robinson, a really remarkable lad for 18. He will go far, I'm sure. He is the son of a deceased rector of St Barnabas, Klerk Nek road, and his mother is travelling too (in the cabin section). Frank is in D3, and we have had some extremely interesting conversations and have exchanged some confidences. He is one of the best Christians of the whole bunch – and that is saying much.

Now I think I have given you a fairly complete picture of what life on board the *Mauretania* has been like, at least as far as the limits of a letter allow. When I return I shall perhaps be able to fill in some of the gaps.

You will know I have been thinking much about you all every day, as I know you have been thinking of me. As the old hymn says: "Though sundered far, by faith we meet, Around one common Mercy Seat!". So goodbye for now. God bless you all. All my love, and many oxos to you all.

Monday, 24.9.45 2 p.m. I didn't expect to be writing you on board on this day or at this time! Our hopes were dashed yesterday when the Skipper broadcast that owing to wind we could not venture up the Mersey Estuary and would lie outside until today. Since then we have been in doubt about our chances of getting away today (I won't tell you what gloomy prognostications the SP indulged in!). However, all doubt has now been dispelled by the orders I have just this minute heard to the Troops – 'parade at once with kit': Three cheers! We are to be alongside at 4 p.m., says the person who always has inside information (he knows a fellow who knows a girl who knows one of the ship's officers – so it must be true!). So here's for good old England. And this is my last word before landing and posting!

Lots of love to you all,

Dad

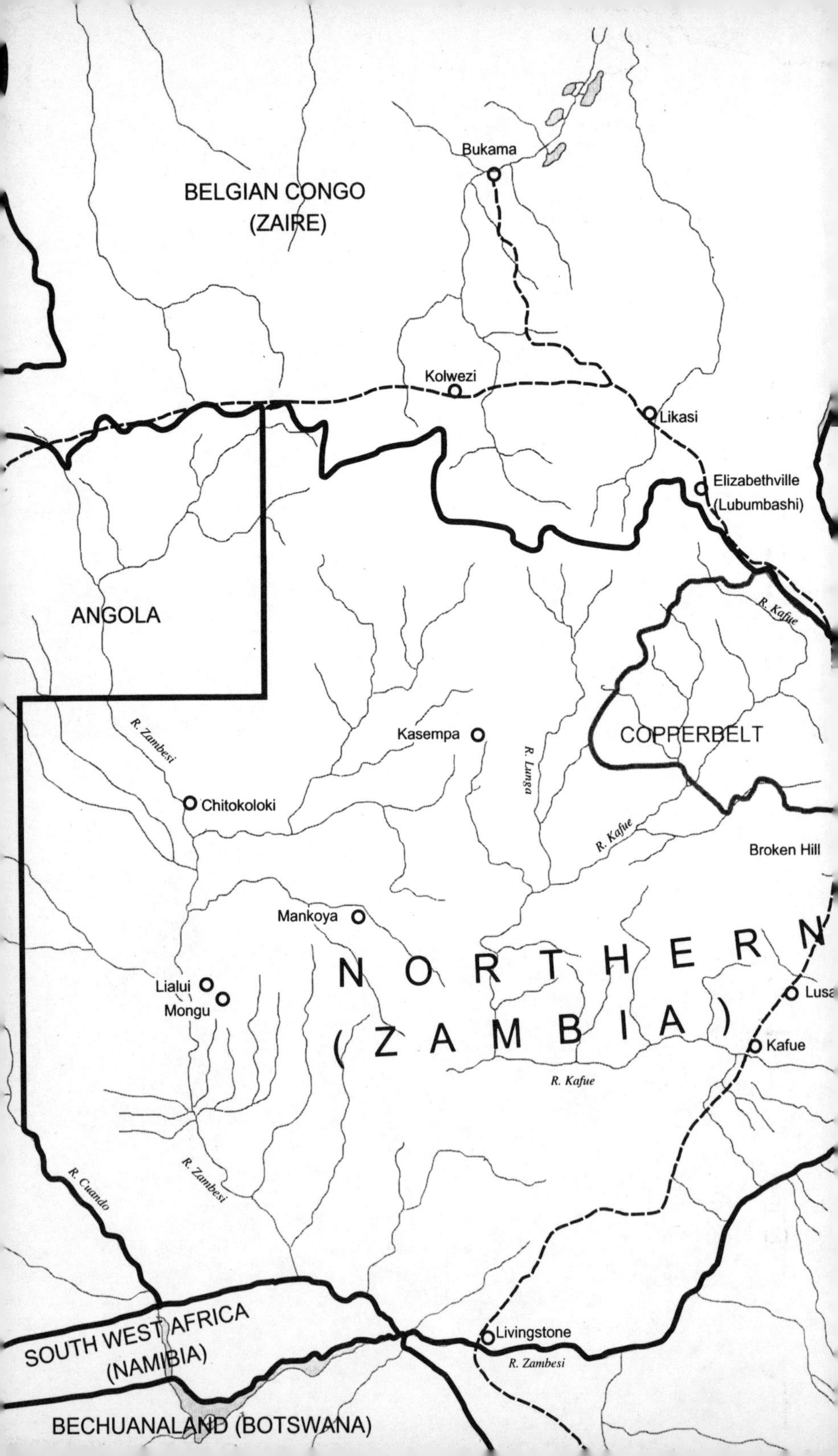
BELGIAN CONGO
(ZAIRE)
Bukama
Kolwezi
Likasi
Elizabethville
(Lubumbashi)
ANGOLA
R. Kafue
COPPERBELT
Kasempa
R. Zambesi
R. Lunga
Chitokoloki
R. Kafue
Broken Hill
Mankoya
NORTHERN
(ZAMBIA)
Lialui
Mongu
Lusa
Kafue
R. Kafue
R. Zambesi
R. Cuando
SOUTH WEST AFRICA
(NAMIBIA)
Livingstone
R. Zambesi
BECHUANALAND (BOTSWANA)